Changing Mi

Changing Mission
Learning from the
Newer Churches

STUART MURRAY

CHURCHES TOGETHER
IN BRITAIN AND IRELAND

Churches Together in Britain and Ireland
Bastille Court
2 Paris Garden
London SE1 8ND

www.ctbi.org.uk

ISBN 085169 305 9
Published 2006

Further copies are available from:
CTBI Publications, 4 John Wesley Road, Werrington,
Peterborough PE4 6ZP

Telephone: 01733 325002

Fax: 01733 384180

Cover designed by Makar Publishing Production
from the series design by Church House Publishing

Produced and typeset in 10.5 on 13pt Palatino
by Makar Publishing Production, Edinburgh

Printed and bound by Cromwell Press

To friends and colleagues in Urban Expression

Contents

Foreword by Revd Terry Tennens

Where are we?

What on earth is going on among the churches of Britain and Ireland at the beginning of this, the 21st century? These are some of the terms used to enable Christians to re-engage with people today in the contemporary mission paradigm: church in the pub; church in the leisure centre; church on Wednesday nights instead of Sundays; emerging church, fresh and re-expressions of church!

Fundamentally, the question remains 'what is church?' Stuart Murray helps us explore the answers to this key question.

What's happening 'out there'?

In *Changing Mission* Stuart Murray assists us in navigating our times by providing a large screen display of a fast developing scene. However, we are provided not simply with the big picture, but also with multi-screen options to dig deeper in specific areas: from church planting to post-Christendom; from postcards from the edge to the new monasticism.

Stuart provides narrative, analysis and questions for the reader to reflect further in this crucial area of being God's missionary people for today.

Why Changing Mission?

Here in one volume is a resource enabling people to assess for themselves answers to the question of changing church and/or changing mission.

This book is relevant to the pioneer church planter – it provides a compass point for reflection, since pioneers are usually action orientated by nature. Certainly in the Building Bridges of Hope (BBH) mission accompaniment scheme, our accompaniers to emerging churches have been appreciated for sticking with the burning questions, difficult issues and challenging values of the world today. Also, on a more practical level, pioneer leaders are over-burdened with so much going on. Finding space to reflect and listen to others, to God and to oneself is the biggest challenge.

However, this book is equally relevant to those in a more traditional church setting who are just beginning to ask the question: what is God calling us to be and to do for this time? Here you will find hints, stories and questions to prod and pull you to discern the next steps for you. This might be visiting some of the stories mentioned, or using the bibliography and website directory to find others to speak to, who have embarked on the journey of transition to the mission imperative.

We have discovered in BBH that, whether you are part of an 'inherited' church seeking to re-engage in mission, or you're experiencing fresh expressions of church, the accompaniment of the skilful and supportive outsider, in our terms the 'mission accompanier', is critical to the long term transition and navigation of the choppy waters of the 21st century.

The Challenge of Changing Mission

Finally, we are those that believe in the God of change, who makes every day brand new, who creates afresh the seasons and imagines new possibilities in which Christ comes afresh to us each day. We are those for whom the work of the Spirit of God is about the transformation of all life and for whom the church is called as a servant in the task of God's mission.

Changing Mission will edify and worry some people, and release and challenge others. It will empower Christians to avoid simply falling for the old trick of an attractive new product falsely promising to solve all the problems in our churches.

Throughout this book, Stuart Murray takes us back to God and the call of service and discipleship. This is costly and adventure-some – great courage is demanded of us to be Christ's people for our time. Let's not forget that God goes ahead of us – this journey will be about discovering and encountering life at every turn!

Revd Terry Tennens
Director, Building Bridges of Hope

www.ctbi.org.uk
http://buildingbridges.blogspot.com

Acknowledgements

This book has profited from the help of many people. I am grateful for the privilege of hearing the stories of emerging church pioneers and church planters, for connections friends and colleagues have provided, and for perceptive insights in articles, books, presentations and conversations. I have acknowledged these wherever possible, but sometimes I could not recall the source of particular comments. Please accept my apologies – and my thanks – if you spot a pearl of wisdom you recognise!

My thanks especially to those who read some or all of the manuscript and whose comments prompted revisions that improved the final product: Alan Kreider, Anna Ratcliff, Wale Hudson Roberts, Peter Brierley and, not least, my wife Sian.

The book is dedicated to courageous and creative friends and colleagues in *Urban Expression*, an emerging inner-city church planting initiative (mentioned in various chapters).

1

Learning from the Newer Churches

What are we talking about?

There is no consensus yet about what language to use. Some discuss 'new ways of being church'; others prefer 'emerging church'; a recent Anglican report describes 'fresh expressions of church'; further contenders include 'future church', 'church next' or 'the coming church'.

Nor is there any agreed scheme for classifying what is emerging on the edges of more familiar forms of church. There are trends and patterns, shared values and common features, but whatever is happening appears to be spontaneous rather than centrally organised, fluid rather than settled, diverse rather than uniform, a phenomenon rather than a movement. Emerging churches are motivated by different concerns, espouse diverse convictions and assess their development by varying criteria.

The significance of these developments is hotly debated. Some invest great hope in them, seeing new expressions of church as signs of renewal, evidence of missional engagement with a changing culture, harbingers of church growth in western society beyond unrelenting decline. Others are sceptical, even scathing, suspicious that we have been this way before, convinced that (ecclesially as elsewhere) there is nothing new under the sun, wondering if this is another false dawn or distraction from genuine missional engagement with a post-secular, post-modern, plural culture that has proved remarkably resilient to previous examples of ecclesial reconfiguration. Many are unsure what to think.

Uncertainty about terminology, difficulty in tracking what is happening and reticence about interpreting its implications are understandable. Multiple new expressions of church are emerging, in Britain and elsewhere, but most are small, recently formed and not yet fully developed, let alone capable of demonstrating that they are culturally attuned, missionally potent, theologically aware or spiritually sustainable. These are very early days!

Perhaps, for the moment, we should refrain from describing, categorising and pigeon-holing what is happening. Why do we need to classify and label it? Why rush to judgement before these churches have even fully emerged? Scrutinising experimental forms of church, investing them with unwarranted significance, criticising or lauding them, assigning them agreed places within our intellectual or organisational structures – will they survive such interference or bear the weight they are expected to carry?

And yet we are thirsty for news about emerging churches. I am frequently invited to address conferences, contribute to articles, lecture in theological colleges, suggest books to read and intro- duce ministers on sabbatical to churches they can investigate. A conference on this subject to which I contributed in 2003 involving senior leaders of many denominations in England indicated that interest in emerging churches had penetrated the upper echelons of most ecclesial structures.

Which brings us to this book – commissioned as a contribution to the series published annually by *Building Bridges of Hope*. My instructions are to 'focus on what can be learned from "the newer churches" and from church planting initiatives, and to offer an Anabaptist perspective on these questions.' Given my hesitations about describing, labelling, weighing or publicising new forms of church, why have I accepted this assignment?

What is the point of this book?

Let me clarify at the outset what I will – and will not – attempt to do:

- I will tell stories of emerging churches but I will not reveal their identities or locations unless these are already avail- able via websites or other publications.

- I will classify emerging churches but with the proviso that this is tentative and will be obsolete before this book is published.

- I will reflect on the significance of particular forms of emerging church and on the phenomenon of 'emerging church', but I will offer only provisional assessments and pose mainly open-ended questions.

Let me also explain my involvement in church planting and, more recently, emerging churches. After twelve years as a church planter in London I taught church planting at Spurgeon's College for nine years. Since 2000 I have been a trainer/consultant under the auspices of the Anabaptist Network, working primarily with those involved in urban mission, church planting and emerging churches (in Britain and other western nations). I initiated and direct *Urban Expression*, a mission agency stimulating and sustaining creative urban church planting,[1] and I have spent increasing time over the past five years with emerging churches and individuals involved in these.

And let me identify my convictions and why I agreed to write this book. I believe the church in western culture is in trouble, struggling to adjust to the end of Christendom, persistent decline and social marginality.[2] I don't believe revival is imminent or that there is a quick-fix solution to these difficulties. I anticipate serious denominational disintegration and continuing decline over the next thirty years. I am unsure whether some emerging churches are distractions or a work of the Spirit. I don't believe the way forward lies either with inherited or emerging forms of church but a symbiotic partnership between these. I believe the challenges we face are primarily theological and missiological rather than ecclesiological, but that our responses will impact the shape, location and ethos of the church.

So I write as a practitioner, missiologist, mentor, researcher and trainer, who has not written off the inherited church and its capacity for renewal, but who welcomes the emergence of fresh expressions of church and wants to facilitate mutually helpful conversations between those involved in different forms of church. This book aims to encourage and resource such conversations. I am taking the risk of introducing some emerging churches to a wider audience, reflecting on their significance and raising questions for inherited and emerging churches. What follows is provisional and exploratory. My hope is that it will stimulate conversations, theological reflection, mutual respect, further experimentation[3] and risk-taking.

I write primarily for Christians in inherited churches, rather than those in emerging churches. Hopefully, some of the latter will read this book, find its reflections helpful and respond to the invitation to engage in dialogue with others. But this book is an invitation to the vast majority of Christians who are still in inherited churches to watch the margins, listen to the pioneers and forge mutually enriching friendships.

What language shall we use?

Thus far I have used 'emerging church' for experimental expressions of church and 'inherited church' for more familiar forms. I will generally use this terminology rather than other proposals for several reasons:

- 'New ways of being church' sounds dismissive of 'old ways', which are by implication obsolescent or worse. I am not yet persuaded this is a legitimate judgement.

- Terms like 'future church', 'church next' and 'the coming church' similarly imply that a new era, of which emerging churches are early signs, is arriving that will consign to history inherited forms of church.

- All these terms sound presumptuous for experimental approaches that have not yet proven themselves sustainable or preferable to older models.

- 'New ways of being church' fails to recognise how much has actually been inherited from the past (consciously or unconsciously); it may suggest more radical discontinuity than is appropriate.

- 'Inherited church' is less value-laden than alternatives like 'traditional', 'established' or 'mainstream'.

- 'Fresh expressions of church', for which justification is offered in *Mission-shaped Church*,[4] is an attractive alternative to 'emerging church' but may give the impression of only superficial changes to style, structure and the public face of the church.

- 'Emerging church' risks being interpreted passively as observers watch from a distance to see what might emerge, but it has advantages: it makes no huge claims, indicates gradual and unfinished developments, presupposes a past from which something is emerging, reflects the bottom-up grass-roots nature of what is emerging and conveys the lack of coordination or strategic leadership.

The point of this discussion is not to champion particular phraseology but to highlight problems of definition in an amorphous and fluid area of study and to acknowledge concerns about assumptions and attitudes. The use of 'emerging church' is intended to pre-empt both judgmental attitudes towards inherited churches and over-optimistic assessments of what has not yet fully emerged.

But is it helpful, whatever language we use, to focus on church rather than the mission of God in which the church is invited to share? This is a concern many have about the interest in emerging church. I am suspicious this interest could be another example of rearranging ecclesiastical furniture (or watching others do this) and avoiding the more costly and urgent challenge of engaging in holistic mission in contemporary society.

So I am grateful for the title of this book – *Changing Mission* – which was chosen by those who commissioned it to complement the titles of earlier and forthcoming books in the series. Although our focus will be on the emerging church, this title encourages reflection on the missional impact and implications of emerging forms of church.

What about the 'New Churches'?

The book's subtitle, however, introduces another term – *Learning from the Newer Churches*. This immediately provokes the question: newer than what? It alerts us to the problem of using terms like 'new' to describe movements that will age and be superseded by 'newer' developments. The ugly term 'post-modern' is the result of a similar problem with 'modern'!

The emerging churches we will encounter are certainly newer than inherited forms of church that comprise the major denominations, but they are also newer than churches that 'emerged' in the 1970s and 1980s. These were first called 'House Churches' and then, as many of them grew, 'New Churches'. This was an uninspired and uninspiring designation (which, as usual in church history, participants did not choose); we now require the term 'newer' to distinguish emerging churches from that older 'new' movement.

Again, this is not just a question of semantics. For many (though not all) in the New Churches believed and taught that their 'new way of being church' would supersede older models and enable the whole church to reach maturity in readiness for the return of Christ and the great revival that would precede this. Ecclesial creativity marked the movement's early years, with fresh thinking about worship, spiritual gifts, healing, leadership, community and much else. Rapid growth ensued – more impressive than anything yet in the emerging church scene – and expectations were heightened of further expansion, although some recognised that the increase was mainly through 'transfer growth' rather than conversion.

By the mid-1990s, however, stagnation and decline were replacing growth in many parts of the movement and disillusionment was increasing. The promised revival appeared elusive, ecclesial creativity had dried up, many supposedly 'new churches' seemed disappointingly similar to older churches (some of which were thriving rather than fading away as predicted), transfers were occurring in the opposite direction and the movement seemed to have lost focus and impetus. It was looking increasingly like an attempt to revive an old model of church rather than a new model. There were and are exceptions to this analysis as some New Churches continue to thrive, but most of these have reverted to traditional ecclesial patterns and practices.

Some New Churches are currently negotiating the turbulence movements experience when the pioneers face impending retirement and must hand over to younger leaders. This is a testing time when foundations laid are put under considerable strain and the future health or survival of the movement is determined. The transition can be painful and fraught with difficulties, jeopardising what has been achieved and breaking long-established relationships. The difficulties are exacerbated if younger leaders have little theological training and limited experience of other ways of being church. This can create insecurity and result in safety-first entrenchment or a desperate search for the next 'new thing'.

How the New Churches negotiate this difficult stage and whether they will experience renewal and further growth will not be clear for several years, but their experience already holds lessons for 'newer' emerging churches:

- Ecclesial creativity is hard to sustain. Churches generally revert to default positions or regard as sacrosanct forms developed at a particular stage. This is not surprising:

creativity is very tiring. Settled patterns and rituals are needed to sustain communities over the long haul.

- What newer churches pioneer, if it has inherent value, older churches often co-opt for their benefit but at the expense of the distinctive identity of the newer churches. Pioneers may perceive this as either threatening or encouraging.

- What appeared cutting edge in the 1970s looked decidedly passé by the 1990s. The pioneers' children decamped and searched for alternative expressions of church. Pete Ward comments: 'guitars, choruses and informality, whilst in their time being an attempt at relevance, in the 1990s appear to be yesterday's style . . . Plastic chairs were modern, but unfortunately what was modern is no longer in vogue.'⁵ In a rapidly changing culture emerging churches will not keep pace without regularly reinventing themselves.

- New churches can easily confuse culturally attuned approaches to mission, worship and community with transcultural principles invested with biblical authority and unwarranted status. Once we have found 'the New Testament way of being church' it is difficult to adjust!

- The temptation to concentrate on renewing or restoring the church rather than engaging in mission (however defined) is hard to resist but ultimately this will produce ingrown churches that are no more missionally effective than those from which pioneers of newer churches emerged.

- Eschewing theological training and the traditions of inherited churches may protect new churches from 'pollution' but eventually results in weaker and narrower churches. Equally, arrogant and dismissive attitudes towards newer churches deprive inherited churches of much-needed challenge and stimulus.

- Unrealistic expectations in the early years of a new church may produce high initial enthusiasm and commitment but precipitate disillusionment when these expectations are not realised.

Contemporary emerging churches will be immeasurably weaker if they fail to draw on the experience of other emerging churches from recent decades.

How new are new ways of being church?

Many stories told here, and in other books and articles on emerging churches, are very recent. The turn of the millennium sparked an outburst of creativity and activity. We will examine in Chapter 3 reasons for these developments. But Christians in western culture have been seeking alternative models of church and mission for decades. The emergence of New Churches in the 1970s and the emphasis on church planting in the 1990s are not the only precursors of the present wave.

Read, for example, *Alternative Church* by John Vincent (founder of the Urban Theology Unit in Sheffield), in which he introduces various emerging churches and reflects on their significance. This was published in 1976 but has a remarkably contemporary feel.[6]

Trace the emergence of Christian communities during the twentieth century. Some of these flourished and faded; others continue to model forms of spirituality, community and mission that offer alternative possibilities to conventional churches.[7]

Learn the story of hundreds of Caribbean churches in Britain during the 1960s and 1970s and ponder why Christians from the West Indies found many British churches unwelcoming or uncongenial.[8] Caribbean churches were forerunners of a proliferation of mono-ethnic churches in the past fifteen years, especially in London.

From these and other twentieth-century examples of emerging church today's pioneers can receive encouragements and warnings. And Christians in inherited churches can also note that what happens on the ecclesial margins need neither be arrogantly dismissed nor precipitately hailed as salvific: healthy interaction between 'mainstream' and 'margins' is preferable to suspicion and polarisation.

Previous emerging churches did not supplant inherited churches, so 'mainstream' and 'margins' are appropriate terms to describe their impact. But they subverted inherited churches and stimulated renewal. And many churches and communities continued, finding their place within an increasingly crowded ecclesiastical landscape.

So the emerging churches described in this book are new in the sense that they are of recent origin, but the phenomenon of churches emerging around the edges of inherited churches is not new. Indeed, most denominations can trace their origins to the gradual emergence of alternative ways of being church around the fringes of older institutions.

What's wrong with old ways of being church?

Is there any reason to suppose that what is happening today has greater significance than this? Will churches emerging over the coming years have a similarly provocative influence, stimulating inherited churches to review their practice and renew their vision, before either disappearing or becoming younger but increasingly respectable ecumenical partners?

Even if this is what we anticipate, we should watch carefully and allow the pioneers to challenge, trouble and envision us. There are many biblical precedents for God acting and speaking from the margins to renew a sluggish mainstream. We now know the answer to the question – 'can anything good come out of Nazareth?'[9] – but it was not obvious at the time! Ignoring or despising emerging churches is not only arrogant and uncharitable; it could be dangerous.

But might the current upheaval be more significant? Are there different contextual factors to consider? Yes! We will investigate these in Chapter 3 but we can identify them here: an alarming exodus of Christians from inherited churches; the combined impact on the church of post-modernity and post-Christendom; persistent decline in church affiliation, however this is measured; ineffective recruitment of new members; unprecedented failure to transmit the faith to the next generation; and the prospect that several denominations will within thirty years be non-viable in their present form.

It is too early to know whether emerging churches are a peripheral distraction from this demanding agenda or spearheading the church's response. They may remain marginal or become mainstream. Perhaps such language will become redundant in decentred post-modern culture, where claims to being 'mainstream' are regarded as illegitimate power-plays, and in post-Christendom, where all churches are on the margins and new forms of grass-roots ecumenism are emerging.

In the following chapters we will be more attracted to some emerging churches than others, and as the examples multiply so will our questions and objections. We may be tempted to dismiss these stories, either because they are too disturbing or because they do not seem radical enough. We may become defensive of inherited church, in which many of us have invested so much.

This book advocates constructive engagement, rooted in humility, openness and self-awareness, willing to ask hard questions but listening carefully, critical of inherited and emerging patterns, ready to make new friends and attentive to God's Spirit surprising, affirming and challenging us.

John Vincent concluded his tour of alternative churches with warnings to leaders of inherited churches. These bear repeating as we embark on a similar journey:

> Contemporary churchmen – I speak as one of them! – are very good at dismissing new things before they have even been heard, much less encouraged and stayed with and loved. "We've seen it all before," they say: "Just a few odd sects." "Just a few entrepreneurs doing their own thing." "Malcontents who cannot stand church discipline." "The blind leading the blind."
>
> And soon, the ultimate knock-out is delivered. "Will they stand the test of time?"
>
> On other occasions, the opposite tack is tried: "They are really only setting up another church." "They are only the same as we are." "They will become as institutional as we are in the end."
>
> If they are different, they are wrong. If they are like the churches, they are wrong.
>
> Is it too much to say that all these kinds of responses indicate a deep sickness among contemporary Churchmen? "If it's different from what we are, we don't want it. If it's the same as we are, why bother to create it?"
>
> Let us learn to love each other . . . [10]

What has Anabaptism got to do with this?

The final part of my brief – to offer 'an Anabaptist perspective' – immediately raises questions. What is Anabaptism? Are Anabaptist perspectives operative in emerging churches? Why should they be helpful in interpreting what is happening?

Anabaptism (another imposed label) was a sixteenth-century missional movement into a changing culture that resulted in different forms of church emerging. Regarded as heretical and subversive by the inherited churches, both Catholic and Protestant, Anabaptists were persecuted and suppressed. But the Anabaptist tradition survived and during the twentieth century developed into a global network of churches with distinctive perspectives on theological, ethical, ecclesial and missional issues.

Anabaptists were unwelcome in Britain. Some asylum-seekers fleeing persecution in the Netherlands reached London in 1575 but were arrested, imprisoned, interrogated and executed or deported. Among charges brought against them was that of schism – they dared to form unsanctioned churches. In the Christendom era everyone was at least a latent Christian and legally a member of the state church. Anabaptism was threatening because it rejected these assumptions, planted churches free from state control and modelled counter-cultural forms of community and mission.

But in post-Christendom, where such assumptions no longer make sense and inherited approaches are in difficulty, neglected Anabaptist perspectives are startlingly relevant. The Anabaptist tradition has quietly re-entered Britain and Christians from many denominations have found it helpful. Anabaptism, like all traditions, has strengths and weaknesses but it represents a marginalised dimension of European church history whose insights are now appreciated beyond its historic boundaries. The Anabaptist Network began in 1991 to link those interested in Anabaptism and provide further resources. Its core convictions include three statements that are especially relevant to this study:

- Western culture is slowly emerging from the Christendom era when church and state jointly presided over a society in which almost all were assumed to be Christian. Whatever its positive contributions on values and institutions, Christendom seriously distorted the gospel, marginalised Jesus and has left the churches ill-equipped for mission in a post-Christendom culture. As we reflect on this, we are committed to learning from the experience and perspectives of movements such as Anabaptism that rejected standard Christendom assumptions and pursued alternative ways of thinking and behaving.

- The frequent association of the church with status, wealth and force is inappropriate for followers of Jesus and damages our witness. We are committed to exploring ways of being good news to the poor, powerless and persecuted.

- Churches are called to be committed communities of discipleship and mission, places of friendship, mutual accountability and multi-voiced worship that sustain hope as we seek God's kingdom together. We are committed to nurturing and developing such churches, in which young and old are valued, leadership is consultative, roles are related to gifts rather than gender and baptism is for believers.[11]

Are Anabaptist perspectives operative within emerging churches? Many are unaware of this tradition or uninterested in it. Some (such as Urban Expression) draw explicitly and gratefully on Anabaptism. Others become increasingly interested in Anabaptism as they perceive points of contact between this earlier emerging church movement and emerging churches today. Emerging churches grappling with post-Christendom as well as post-modernity are especially likely to find Anabaptism relevant.

Why should Anabaptist perspectives be helpful in interpreting what is happening? It may simply be that Anabaptism provides an unusual angle of vision or lens through which to study the scene. This has been an Anabaptist contribution to many Christians in recent years, providing a different way of looking at the Bible, the life and teaching of Jesus, theological and ethical issues, mission and discipleship. Maybe Anabaptist perspectives (rooted in rejection of the Christendom mindset) can help us interpret the significance of emerging churches for post-Christendom as well as post-modernity.

So, without this becoming obtrusive, I will endeavour to offer 'an Anabaptist perspective' on emerging churches. In a sense I can, of course, do no other since this is the tradition out of which I work and write, but I value the invitation to be explicit about this and to identify my presuppositions. Perhaps I can encourage you to identify the lens through which you will look as you examine the kaleidoscopic scene that is the emerging church in Britain today.

2

The Church Planting Legacy

Church planting: a newly respectable practice

Once a disreputable practice associated with fringe movements and subversive groups (like Anabaptists!), during the 1990s church planting became respectable and widely accepted. A remarkably ecumenical (though mainly evangelical) movement coalesced early in the decade and church planting climbed the agenda until it preoccupied many church leaders and dominated many consultations. A new literature emerged[12], church planting targets were proposed and many new churches were planted. Although some traditions struggle with the ecclesial implications for issues like parochial boundaries and Eucharistic celebration, many denominations now recognise church planting as a vital component of their mission strategy.

During the 1990s practical experience was gained as planters initiated churches in different areas and discovered what worked and what did not. We will reflect on that experience. But we must also examine theological and strategic issues, some of which were inadequately addressed during the 1990s and resulted in some discouraging outcomes. For church planting did not achieve as much as was anticipated. Numerous problems became apparent and there was a steep decline in church planting towards the end of the decade. Many church plants failed. Others replicated struggling models of church. Some grew but only through transfers.

Since the turn of the millenium enthusiasm for church planting has been rekindled, but with greater concern about the kinds of churches planted rather than the numbers of additional churches. The change in terminology from 'church planting' to 'new ways of being church', 'emerging church' or 'fresh expressions of church' is indicative of this shift of emphasis.

Church planting: a persistent necessity

Despite the heightened attention it received during the 1990s, there is nothing new about church planting. Church planting has been occurring since the first century and has taken four main forms:[13]

- *Pioneer planting* is the practice of establishing churches in areas previously unreached by the gospel but now being evangelised and discipled. Wherever missionaries have advanced geographically this form of church planting has been undertaken. This form of church planting is the least controversial.

- *Replacement planting* is the practice of establishing churches in areas where churches had previously been planted but no longer exist, due to factors such as persecution or decline. Church history contains many instances of regions once evangelised needing to be re-evangelised. Given the ebbs and flows of church history, this practice too is relatively widely accepted.

- *Sectarian planting* is the practice of establishing more churches in areas where churches already exist to express and embody distinctive doctrinal, spiritual or ecclesiological convictions. Although 'sectarian' can be used sociologically without the negative overtones it often carries, this form of church planting is highly controversial. Sixteenth-century Anabaptist church planting was sectarian.

- *Saturation planting* is the practice of establishing more churches in areas where churches already exist to enhance the churches' ability to engage in mission in these areas. The new churches may differ from existing churches, but these differences tend to be pragmatic rather than ideological. During the final quarter of the twentieth century, in several nations co-operative strategies were developed to harness the resources of many agencies and denominations in co-ordinated church planting campaigns.

During the 1990s all four forms of church planting were operative (if pioneer planting includes planting into new housing developments where there have never previously been churches). Many factors prompted church planting – some were 'pull' factors as mission challenges stirred Christians to action; others were 'push' factors as ecclesial developments encouraged initiatives.

An undoubtedly incomplete list of reasons for church planting includes:

- To replace churches that have closed, leaving some areas relatively under-churched.
- To replace ineffective churches that are not engaged in mission within their community.
- To penetrate contemporary society more effectively by providing churches nearer to where people live.
- To respond to regional or local population increases.
- To relocate Christians to areas of greater spiritual and social need.
- To offer denominations opportunities to experiment with different forms of church and mission.
- To help denominations adapt to a rapidly changing culture.
- To provide more options for connecting with people beyond the churches.
- To develop specialised or targeted churches.
- To encourage disaffected Christians to reconnect.
- To create younger churches that tend to grow more effectively.
- To release space in full church buildings by deploying members from growing congregations.
- To provide more Christians with opportunities for service and leadership.
- To release faith and energy as Christians become actively involved in a mission initiative.
- To release tension within a congregation by allowing those with divergent visions to explore these separately.

These reasons beg questions that cannot be addressed here. They indicate that church planting is multi-faceted, motivated by different factors and capable of addressing crucial missiological and ecclesial issues which denominations and local churches face in contemporary society.

Strategic discussions about whether planting is appropriate in particular contexts are crucial before embarking on demanding and frequently risky ventures, but church planting *per se* is a persistent necessity. Christians have responded to the challenges of changing mission frontiers, housing developments and cross-cultural ministry by planting churches.

In a context of church decline and closures, the only alternative to church planting is to abandon responsibility for the spiritual welfare of communities in various parts of Britain. And in a plural and rapidly evolving culture, it requires considerable faith to believe denominations can adapt to these social changes and an increasingly diverse constituency without planting new churches.

Inherited churches have some degree of flexibility and cannot evade the challenge to stretch out beyond their comfort zones, but the illusion that existing churches can effectively incarnate the gospel to everyone in a multi-everything society must be shattered. If our calling is to incarnate the gospel rather than invite people to become like us in order to encounter the Christ we follow, church planting is an essential component.

Church members had tried hard, but people from the estate felt uncomfortable in the parish church. They used it for weddings and funerals but waited outside until the last moment and shot out once the service finished. Invitations to social events and special services fell on deaf ears. The few who did come did not return. It was time to face reality: the parish church had its own culture that was alien to those who lived on the estate. Their notice board proclaimed 'All Welcome' – and they meant it. But people from the estate did not feel they belonged.

The next five years were a roller-coaster: deciding to plant a new church on the estate; researching a community they thought they knew but which had thrown up surprising findings; appointing a curate to pioneer the new church and their joy at obtaining a flat for her on the estate; tentative beginnings in the homes of two estate families; the long period when nothing seemed to be happening and questions were asked about whether to continue; growing friendships and growing interest in the gospel; the first service in the community centre, curtailed by the caretaker wanting to lock up earlier than agreed; the battle to persuade the authorities not to relocate the curate; the stormy PCC meeting when some people suddenly understood that those who were attending services on the estate would not be expected eventually to attend the 'proper' church.

The future of the church plant is uncertain – though the same could be said for the 500-year-old parish church. But a Christian community now worships on the estate in a style and location that residents find accessible. Members of this community are deeply involved in the local school, help run a toy library and are welcome in the homes of many neighbours. The caretaker has given them a key and trusts them to lock up the community centre!

Church planting is not about denominational aggrandisement or local entrepreneurial initiatives. It is about re-contextualising the gospel into segments of contemporary society among whom inherited churches are struggling to make their message audible or visible. Understood in this way, any gap between 'church planting' and 'emerging church' begins to disappear, but this anticipates an issue to which we will shortly turn.

Church planting is concerned about planting *more* churches where these are needed, but even more about planting *new* churches. Anabaptist missiologists and church planters especially have highlighted this challenge in recent years.[14] Creative church planting (rather than replicating existing churches) keeps denominations and local congregations open to the challenges of mission, alert to cultural developments and aware of new ecclesial possibilities. Such church planting offers laboratories for the Spirit to inspire fresh discoveries about the relationship between gospel and culture, church and kingdom, spirituality and mission.

However, this summary of the role and potential of church planting benefits from hindsight. Church planting was not generally interpreted in this way during the 1990s (though there were exceptions). In the heady atmosphere of planting congresses, expectations were high that many churches could be planted by the turn of the millenium and questions of missiology and ecclesiology were largely ignored. So we turn next to a brief survey of church planting in the 1990s.[15]

Church planting: an encouraging and disappointing decade

Church planting attained a high profile as one aspect of the Decade of Evangelism to which many denominations subscribed. Several denominations endorsed church planting within their mission strategies and invested resources in training, deploying and supporting planters. *Challenge 2000* advocated, tracked and co-ordinated church planting. Although some denominations and New Church streams with active planting strategies did not participate in this initiative, planting was generally co-operative: a national consortium emerged, inspired by and linked with the international DAWN (Disciple a Whole Nation) movement.

Critics were unimpressed by the re-packaged church growth ideology some detected, concerned about the narrowly evangelical agenda and lack of holistic mission evident in many planting initiatives, and wary that other legitimate dimensions of mission and ministry were being swamped by this current fad. Limited missiological reflection and failure to contextualise a strategy adopted from another cultural setting[16] undermined the movement. But despite these deficiencies, church planting achieved recognition as a legitimate and desirable mission strategy.

Hundreds of new churches were planted across Britain. Precise figures are elusive because of the unofficial nature of much planting in denominations that operate on the basis of congregational autonomy and because different criteria were used to decide when to designate an initiative as a 'church plant'; but about 1900 churches opened in England. Some denominations saw more churches planted in the 1990s than in any previous decade of the twentieth century.

The Salvation Army's Bob Halliday reported in December 2001:

From its origins in 1865 until 1905 the Salvation Army functioned as a mission organisation rather than a church, was pragmatic rather than theoretical, had a passion to 'save the world', and was attractive to people fired with this vision.

Initially, converts joined local churches, but when they did not stay, the pragmatic response was to plant suitable churches. The Salvation Army's success was based on releasing young people to plant churches. However, in 1905, there was a shift from being a mission organisation to becoming a corporate structure.

In the early 1990s, a church planting programme was initiated: seventy church plants were initiated, of which thirty-three survived. Sadly, many represented 'more of the same' rather than fresh expressions of church. Nevertheless, there was more church planting in the Salvation Army between 1985 and 1995 than at any time since the shift from mission organisation to corporate structure in 1905.

For advocates of church planting, there was much to celebrate. Despite weaknesses and shortcomings, new churches were planted, existing churches were encouraged and renewed by participating in such activities, and important lessons were learned (from failures and successes) about how to plant churches effectively. Experience was shared in conferences, books, training courses and conversations. Throughout this period I was directing the church planting course at Spurgeon's College and had the privilege of training church planters, reflecting with them on what they were doing and learning, rejoicing in progress and helping them work through problems. I applaud unreservedly the courage, creativity and passion of these men and women.

But, as the 1990s wore on, significant difficulties began to be recognised within the planting movement. The unofficial but influential goals within many denominations for the number of churches to be planted by 2000 were well out of reach. Serious misjudgements had been made about the capacity for church planting. Contrary to expectations, church planting was not reversing decline or stimulating overall church growth. Although some 1900 churches were opened in England, at least 2700 were closed.

Furthermore, many new churches failed to thrive. Some closed after years of struggle (the closure rate is hard to discern, but may be as high as 50 per cent). Many remained small, weak and financially dependent on others and made little impact on the community they set out to serve. And most of the churches that grew numerically were effective primarily in reaching those with previous church links. Dormant faith was renewed and individuals who had left other churches were restored, but few churches attracted individuals or communities without previous church connections.

There were also strategic problems. Planting in most denominations relied heavily on the initiative of local congregations and their entrepreneurial leaders. Consequently, churches were often not planted in areas of greatest need but areas with the strongest churches and greatest resources of personnel and finance. And, as we have indicated, there was limited reflection on the nature of mission in contemporary culture and the kinds of churches required. Although there was some creativity and contextualisation, many plants were clones of existing churches rather than grasping the opportunity to develop new forms of church in diverse cultural contexts.

By 1996 it was evident that enthusiasm was flagging and planting was slowing down. Church planting was harder than had been anticipated and took longer. Churches that had planted new churches could not plant out again as quickly as had been hoped, nor were recently planted churches ready to reproduce as soon as would be necessary if the ambitious targets were to be met. The envisaged planting *movement* did not materialise (*Challenge 2000* disintegrated by mid-decade), and it was clear inadequate attention had been given to how newly planted churches would mature. Leadership was a particularly critical issue: there were simply not enough leaders available with the skills, experience and training needed for effective church planting.

There was a significant human cost, as planters struggled not only with the normal demands of planting churches but with unrealistic expectations and uncertainty about where to turn for help. Few denominations had adequate support structures for church planters. During this period a steady stream of disappointed and discouraged planters passed through my office – angry, tearful, stoic, resentful, struggling to make sense of their experience. Some have worked through these experiences and have moved into fruitful areas of ministry; others have not yet recovered.

He sat in my office, weeping openly. He was in his 30's and had been leading a church planting team in a town in the south of England. Seven years earlier this team of 23 people had been commissioned by their church to plant a new church in another part of the town.

They had worked hard, prayed hard, tried everything they had heard about in planting conferences and read about in the books. But seven years on there were 22 of them, exhausted, disillusioned and making no impact on the community.

The sending church had offered little help over the years and seemed uninterested in them. He really wanted to quit, but he had been so sure God had called them to plant a new church that this felt like disobedience.

Why had nothing happened? What should he do now?

At the same time, some were starting to discuss missiological issues more vigorously. Were truly missional churches being planted? Indeed, what was a missional church? Should denominations address this question before attempting to plant more churches? This was the decision taken by the Assemblies of God, whose vibrant planting strategy had foundered by mid-decade. Wisely they paused to lay firmer missiological foundations. Planters were exploring broader missional issues than at the start of the decade.

Fresh thinking about ecclesiology was also developing. Rather than assuming church planting meant 'more of the same', many were asking what kinds of churches needed to be planted. The language of 'new ways of being church' was beginning to be heard, both among church planters and in other groups that had not been involved in church planting or attracted to the ethos and ideology of the planting movement.

Pausing to reflect was vital – but it meant church planting lost momentum. Fewer churches were planted in the second half of the decade and church planting slipped back down denominational agendas. As interest in 'seeker services', *Alpha* and 'cell church' grew, it seemed as though church planting might fade without achieving its potential to catalyse the experimentation and missiological reflection that remains vital in our post-modern, post-Christendom society.

Church planting: a shift in emphasis

Where are we now? The resurgence of church planting since the beginning of the new century is nowhere near the level of the early 1990s yet, but a new wave of planting may be approaching. One factor stimulating this is the realisation in some regions that hundreds of thousands of new homes are to be built in areas without churches of any kind. Another is the active encouragement of young planters by senior denominational leaders, who are convinced their future depends on such initiatives.

But conversations about church planting are more measured and sober than ten years ago. Advocates and practitioners are more aware of the pitfalls and demands, although many of us remain passionately convinced about the persistent necessity of planting. There is greater readiness to learn from the experience of others, which hopefully will mean fewer casualties. A frequent frustration in the 1990s was listening to struggling planters who might have avoided common problems simply by talking to their peers. However, since most literature on church planting produced in the 1990s is now out of print or out of date, an urgent requirement for effective planting is the development of new training materials. Denominational leaders also face important choices about training priorities, the allocation of resources and provision of support networks.

Different models of planting are also developing. Church planting is less dependent on the entrepreneurial 'mother-daughter' methodology that dominated the 1990s. For many people church planting was equated with this model, whereby a thriving local congregation took the initiative, commissioned a fairly large group of its members to form the core of a new congregation nearby and offered support and encouragement until the new church was ready for independence. Although this model has strengths, it also has serious weaknesses: it can only be used by larger churches and not often without damaging the church; it usually produces clones rather than new expressions of church; and it does not result in churches being planted strategically. Recently an encouraging diversification of planting models has been evident, with the deployment of cross-cultural mission teams and the development of regional strategies, alongside more spontaneous initiatives.

But what about ecumenical church planting? Especially in the context of new housing developments, an ecumenical approach to planting has much to commend it (and may be essential if developers are to offer sites for church buildings). And yet ecumenical planting has a poor track record. Research in the 1990s suggested it was ineffective and fraught with difficulties. Common problems included complicated governance structures, unclear vision, concentration on internal dynamics and a tendency to focus on buildings rather than mission. Attempts to galvanise initiatives at diocesan, association or circuit level often failed to ignite local enthusiasm and foundered.

These continue to be serious concerns that anyone considering ecumenical strategies needs to ponder carefully. But lessons have been learned from the struggles of the past decade. Reports are arriving of strategic ecumenical church planting that is less bureaucratic, more missional, more creative and more contextual, with a healthier relationship between those on the ground and denominational gate-keepers.

The other positive development, emerging from the pause for reflection noted above, is greater sensitivity to the mission context within which churches are planted. Most planters are reflecting seriously on the post-modern, post-Christendom, urbanised, secular/religious, fragmented and networked society we have become. Rather than assuming current expressions of church are adequate for all sectors of this complex context, many are pioneering different ways of being church to relate to those who are culturally as well as geographically distant from the churches.

Church planting: a resource for learning

This missiological and contextual approach to planting is one source of the current interest in new forms of church. Indeed, the language of church planting has in many places been superseded by terms like 'new ways of being church', 'emerging church' and 'fresh expressions of church'. The Anglican report, *Mission-shaped Church*, is both an update on church planting since the previous report in 1994 and a survey of fresh expressions of church that now need to be examined in any report on church planting.[17]

But the emerging church scene should not be interpreted simply as an outgrowth of the 1990s planting movement. Some of those involved in emerging churches perceive themselves as church planters and acknowledge their roots in the planting movement. Many others, though, would not define themselves as planters and are critical of the planting movement for its tendency to clone, its fixation on numerical growth and its modernistic ethos. They are inclined to regard planting initiatives of the past decade as ill-conceived and futile attempts to repackage and franchise forms of church that are not working.

Nor is the enthusiastic endorsement of fresh expressions of church in *Mission-shaped Church* and elsewhere shared by all church planters. Some are concerned that many emerging churches are not missional and suspect this whole phenomenon may be self-indulgent and introspective, offering new options for Christians rather than engaging with those beyond the churches.

The relationship between church planting and the emerging church we will investigate in the following chapters, then, is complex with suspicion on both sides.

My own conviction is that church planters and those involved in the emerging church need each other if churches are to emerge that can engage creatively and contextually in contemporary culture. The missional cutting edge of church planting (at its best) and the ecclesial imagination of emerging church (at its best) need to be combined. Even those involved in emerging churches who prefer not to think of themselves as church planters could learn much from the failures and achievements of planters during the past decade. They may be involved in different forms of church and operating on the basis of different values and expectations, but there are transferable principles from which they could learn. Church planters, too, need to listen carefully to those who are exploring alternative ways of being church if they are to avoid slipping back into the cloning technology of the 1990s.

And the inherited church – denominations, regional bodies, local congregations and training institutions – needs to draw on the experiences of church planters and learn from the 1990s. In the following chapters we will examine lessons inherited churches might learn from emerging churches, but there are important lessons from the planting movement that should be learned before consigning church planting to history and sitting hopefully at the feet of emerging churches.

Based on a consultation in December 2001 with representatives from most of the main denominations and some New Church streams (and augmented by subsequent conversations with representatives from those not present), George Lings (the director of the Church Army's Sheffield Centre) and I compiled a report that assessed what had happened in the 1990s and summarised learning points for the future.[18]

Without repeating material contained in that report, several points can be underlined:

- Let the mission context be primary, shaping the churches that emerge, rather than imposing models of church on communities.

- Think demographically as well as geographically, responding to the mixed neighbourhood/network nature of relationships in contemporary society.

- Be creative in the forms of church planted and in the planting models used to establish them. Think outside the box.

- If ecumenical planting is attempted, find lightweight, provisional and flexible working processes that do not distract from the primary purpose of mission.

- Develop a healthy balance between strategic planning and local initiative so that planting can be responsive but also responsible.

- Choose suitable leaders and provide the kind of support, accountability and opportunity for theological reflection that liberates rather than inhibits.

- Make use of mentors, coaches and consultants and develop learning networks so that church planters are not isolated. The 'accompanying' model developed by *Building Bridges of Hope* could be helpful for many church planters.[19]

- Be patient and realistic about the longer timeframe required for genuinely missional church planting than for cloning.

Church planting: a continuing challenge

Church planting does not appeal, as a concept or in practice, to some Christians. The terminology causes difficulties for some who have a more sacramental or institutional ecclesial perspective. Catholic and Anglo-Catholic friends have explained to me that, while they welcome ecclesial creativity and new mission initiatives, church planting is not language with which they are comfortable. To my surprise, however, a Greek Orthodox friend, who had previously reported a similar reaction in his constituency, recently said that church planting language was now being used. In England, the Orthodox are sectarian!

Church planting also poses problems for denominations whose identity involves the notion of being a national church operating through a parish system. Although many recognise that parish boundaries are often anachronistic[20] and accept that communities are frequently served by churches of different denominations as well as the 'parish' church, deep commitment to the parochial idea persists. Attempting to plant across parish boundaries either causes enormous offence or requires seemingly interminable negotiation. Claiming one is planting a 'network church' rather than a 'neighbourhood church' has been a useful solution in recent years,[21] but a more comprehensive re-think may be required.

The impending reality is that the parish structure is facing collapse. Reorganisation, the development of team ministry and mergers of churches have enabled it to survive thus far, but declining congregations and limited numbers of ministers suggest that available resources will soon be stretched beyond breaking point. Conversations with Church of England and Church of Scotland ministers indicate that, while officially these churches remain committed to national parish ministry, the demise of the system is now being whispered about. This prospect may be greeted with dismay, but what is required is an honest and courageous appraisal of the situation, acceptance that our context is one of cross-cultural mission rather than pastoral responsibility for latent Christians, and strategic redeployment of personnel and resources. Among other things, this is likely to involve 'replacement' church planting.[22]

Church planting is not a panacea, nor will it be appropriate in

27

every context. But it remains a key component in the development of strategies that will enable churches to engage courageously and creatively with post-modern and post-Christendom culture.

This context requires both church renewal and church planting, and the most effective approach will be a symbiotic relationship between these strategies. The planting required is not establishing more churches of the kind we already have, for many of these are declining and most are struggling to impact a changing culture. Nor is it the development of new churches that will leave existing churches untouched or, worse, drain them of resources and hinder them from exploring new ways of responding to their culture.

The strategic response to the challenges of post-modernity and post-Christendom is *both* to plant new churches that engage creatively with this culture *and* to transform existing churches into missionary congregations able to contextualise the gospel in this culture. The most effective route towards these two goals is surely to find ways of learning together. Church planters can draw on the accumulated wisdom of inherited churches – traditions that may offer vital clues for effective planting. And leaders of inherited churches can learn from the experimentation and creativity of pioneering church planters as they explore fresh ways of engaging with a changing culture.

Planting churches in partnership with (rather than in isolation from) existing churches offers several benefits in a changing culture:

- It provides denominations with opportunities to experiment without unduly threatening existing congregations. Attempts to introduce changes too quickly into many inherited churches will risk damaging them.

- It provides opportunities for church members eager to explore new forms of mission and church, who may otherwise become frustrated by the pace of change and the level of resistance. Planting allows them to develop new forms of mission and explore different expressions of church without needing to carry existing congregations with them.

- It provides a context within which risks can be taken while pastoral support is maintained. Not all planting will succeed and links with inherited churches provide support to those who are disappointed. It is irresponsible to deploy church planters in a demanding environment in which as many may fail as succeed without providing appropriate support before, during and after the planting initiative.

- It provides space for reflection and sharing missiological and ecclesiological insights. Initiatives that fail are opportunities for learning important lessons. Those that succeed and grow are models that might be influential elsewhere. But in both cases – failure or success – lessons learned from church planting can be shared with inherited churches. These may then be willing to embrace some changes themselves and take further steps towards becoming missionary congregations. In the meantime, our more radical and creative leaders will be able to pioneer on behalf of the whole church.

Church planting, then, has the capacity not only to increase the number of churches but also to be a catalyst for renewal. In a changing culture, reflection on the task and shape of the church is a continuing challenge. Planting a new church is a wonderful opportunity to engage in this process. But cloning existing models represents a missed opportunity for ecclesiological renewal and missiological creativity; and planting new kinds of churches in isolation represents a diminished opportunity to stimulate renewal and creativity in inherited churches.

Church planting perceived as 'pioneering on behalf of the whole church' may be the most appropriate way of conceiving its contribution to mission in a post-modern and post-Christendom culture. But this contribution will only be effective if there is within inherited churches readiness, not only to offer support and legitimation to planters, but to learn from them and allow inherited forms of church to be challenged and renewed. And if emerging churches, though understandably reluctant to designate what they are doing as church planting, could also draw on the experience of church planters, this could be a very fruitful process of mutual learning.

3

Encountering Emerging Church

Postcards from the edge

Responding to invitations to reflect with church leaders on the emerging church, I often offer a 'Postcards from the Edge' session, in which I present snapshots of emerging churches I have encountered in Britain and other western nations – some quite exotic, others not that different from familiar models.

I do not only choose models to which I am personally drawn. Nor do I concentrate on success stories. And (for reasons explained in Chapter 1) I give limited information about where these churches are unless they are already publicising their existence. The purpose of the session is to give a flavour of what is emerging around the edges of inherited church, or further afield, and on the margins of society.

Different people respond very differently to these stories. Different expressions of church spark their imagination and some begin to make connections with their own context, wondering whether something similar, but maybe not quite the same, could happen there. This is a refreshing change from conferences and consultations where people are searching for – and sometimes being peddled – 'this-is-the-answer' packages and quick-fix programmes to transform or enlarge their congregations.

An attractive feature of the emerging church is the diversity of what is emerging. There are some popular models where I can identify multiple examples of particular expressions of church. But there are also one-offs with no obvious parallels that I have yet discovered. Contrasting 'emerging' and 'inherited' church, although useful for discussion, has serious limitations, some of which we will examine later in this chapter. But one limitation worth noting here is that emerging churches may be as different from one another as from inherited churches.

So let me offer some 'postcards from the edge' to whet your appetite for the next four chapters. Those chapters will concentrate on churches emerging in Britain, so these postcards are from other western societies.

An Australian church planter is establishing a 'church for surfers' on the Gold Coast. Aware that most inherited churches are culturally distant from the surfing community and that Sunday morning is prime surfing time, he knows the style of church needed will be quite different. Asked if a church comprised entirely of surfers is legitimate, he replies that surfers are his target group but the church will not be restricted to them; surfers, too, have families and friends! He wants to see a targeted church emerge, not a homogeneous one.

A church is emerging among homeless people in a city in northwest USA. Originally an initiative of a neighbourhood church, it has attracted a clientele (including several transsexuals) that its sponsoring church has struggled with and so is now independent, although friendship links continue. Eating together is at the heart of church life, with meals prepared by a homeless chef and the menu chosen each week by homeless men and women. The church has a fixed liturgy to ensure there is one element of stability in the lives of those for whom much is unsettled.

Several Lutheran churches in the Danish capital, Copenhagen, offer 'Night Church' between 11pm and 3am to young people who never attend on Sundays but are on the streets during the week. There is no sermon but liturgical worship and opportunities for prayer and conversation. These churches are flourishing and engaging with those who have no other connection with church.

A Protestant church in Aix-en-Provence, France, sometimes replaces its usual Sunday morning service with 'Culte Café Croissant' (coffee-and-croissant worship). This is an occasion for members to invite friends. The church building is laid out as a café and breakfast is

31

served. They sing some worship songs before a short talk, usually a personal testimony, with plenty of opportunity to discuss in a relaxed way round the tables.

A church in New Zealand offering an 'alternative worship' style of meeting starts with a meal together and uses a bar stool as a symbolic place where people can share their stories. It uses mixed media but is fairly low-tech; its core values are community, creativity and participation. The fifteen-minute teaching slot draws on contributions from many church members who have prepared by reflecting during the past week on a text distributed to them.

Why are emerging churches emerging?

These 'postcards from the edge' raise many questions; they also indicate the diversity of emerging churches. Given this diversity, the reasons why new forms of church are emerging will also be varied. Each example is rooted in a particular context and in the stories and yearnings of those involved. Some emerging churches have connections with others and develop in conversation with people on similar journeys. Some have been inspired by hearing the stories of others. But many have begun spontaneously as groups of Christians, unaware of others or the proliferation of emerging churches have started to explore a different way of being church in their own context.

They had told me their story, rather breathlessly, over the past half an hour, trying hard to convey what was happening as they explored a simpler, more organic way of being church in their West Country community.

They were enthusiastic but uncertain – two young couples on a journey with others from inherited church (in this instance a 'New Church') to an emerging church that was not yet fully formed.

Finally, they paused for breath, looked me in the eye and one of them asked: 'Are we completely mad or are any other Christians thinking like us?'

Without attempting to homogenise a very disparate phenomenon, it may be helpful to identify four significant factors in the emergence of new expressions of church. These are overlapping and inter-related but are worth differentiating as different emerging churches are influenced by some of these factors more than others.

Cultural changes

The proliferation of 'post-' words as descriptors of contemporary culture is indicative of a period of cultural transition. 'Post' simply means 'after', and words that employ this prefix convey two messages: 'things are not what they used to be' and 'we are not yet sure where we are heading'.

Claiming that we live in a post-industrial, post-colonial, post-materialist, post-secular, post-technological world (for instance) suggests that familiar social structures, power dynamics, ideologies and ways of thinking have disappeared or are under threat. What will emerge to replace these is far from clear. The use of provisional 'post-' language is necessary in a time of cultural change.

Such language can also be heard in church circles as we grapple with the implications of post-evangelical, post-liberal, post-charismatic or post-denominational Christianity. These labels tell us little about where the church is heading; they merely identify areas of debate and transition.

Emerging churches should be understood within this context of cultural transition and the parallel turbulence within the church. This is not to imply they are simply captive to cultural changes or driven by shifting social patterns. But, as Christians in many times and places have needed to do, they are engaging with social realities and asking important questions about mission and church in a time of change. Some are doing this intuitively and without explicit cultural analysis; others are reflecting deeply on their cultural context.[23]

Three influential aspects of contemporary western culture are worth naming here: *globalisation, urbanisation* and *pluralisation*. In multi-cultural western cities churches of many kinds are emerging, networking with others across the world in a messy form of ecumenism that bypasses inherited structures. Although not all emerging churches are urban, very many are. They are developing alternatives to inherited churches that, designed for a predominantly rural society, were transplanted into suburbia but never entirely made the transition into the cities.

The most popular 'post-' word, of course, is 'post-modern'; this term and all it implies is heard very frequently in emerging church circles.[24] This is not the place to exegete this concept or comment on the multiple meanings and significance ascribed to it, but there is no doubt many emerging churches are, consciously or unconsciously, trying to find ways of incarnating church into post-modern culture. Their attempts to do this challenge inherited churches – whatever their response to particular emerging church models – to question how far they have capitulated to the culture of modernity and to join the search for effective ways of incarnating the gospel into post-modern society.

The speed and complexity of cultural changes in western society require that such reflection is ongoing in all churches (emerging and inherited) if we are not to be left high and dry as cultural tides ebb and flow. Those who think they have discovered a post-modern expression of church may otherwise be discomforted by the 'post-post-modern' shifts some social commentators are now discerning. Many expressions of church currently emerging may be transitional and succeeded by quite different new emerging churches. It might even mean some inherited churches could make a come-back!

Furthermore, in a plural society, influenced by global trends but also retreating into localism,[25] it seems highly unlikely that the limited range of ecclesial expressions that served a more stable and uniform society will be adequate. If we will take seriously our call to incarnate the gospel, no single model of church will suffice. Inherited and emerging churches alike will do well to refrain from implying that their expression of church is universally appropriate.

We should not infer from this discussion that incarnation means simply 'going with the flow' of contemporary culture. An issue we will encounter throughout this book is the interplay between being culturally attuned and counter-cultural. The persistent challenge of the Anabaptist tradition to inherited and emerging churches is to build communities that do not conform to dominant cultural norms but offer embodied alternatives that are both attractive and disturbing.

The end of Christendom

Anabaptists also highlight another 'post-' word that has received far less attention than post-modernity: 'post-Christendom'. The ecclesial diversification that has been occurring over recent decades, of which presently emerging churches are the latest and perhaps most radical expression, would have been unthinkable during most of the Christendom era. Then the church was a dominant social institution, shaping culture rather than responding to cultural changes, precluding and excluding those who dared explore alternative forms of church. For centuries the church perceived itself, and was perceived by others, as a bulwark of stability; any change was slow and incremental.

Assessments of the Christendom era vary enormously. Many regard it as a courageous attempt to incarnate the gospel in European culture and to take responsibility for the application of Christian values and principles across society. Although corruption and coercion damaged the church's credibility, these were flaws in a system that was hugely beneficial for church and society. Others, including most Anabaptists, regard these flaws as inherent rather than incidental, interpret the fourth-century 'Christendom shift' as a disastrous compromise and rejoice in the demise of a system that thrived only by emasculating the gospel, legitimising injustice and transforming a liberating movement into an oppressive institution. There are, of course, other interpretations of Christendom located between these positions.[26]

But the demise of Christendom, however we assess that era, is well advanced in most western societies,[27] and another reason for the emergence of new forms of church is the recognition (even if post-Christendom terminology is unfamiliar) that marginal churches in post-Christendom society cannot operate as they did when the church was central and represented majority culture. *Mission-shaped Church* identifies this as a factor provoking fresh expressions of church and requiring of inherited churches fresh ways of thinking and acting.[28]

Simply to acknowledge that the Christendom era is over is not enough. Anabaptists have urged thorough analysis and critique of the Christendom mindset as a basis for discovering appropriate expressions of church in post-Christendom. This may be a particular contribution the Anabaptist tradition can make to emerging churches, who are familiar with issues arising from post-modernity but have yet to work through the implications of the post-Christendom shift that has influenced their development, whether they realise this or not.

From inherited churches, too, post-Christendom invites responses. If emerging forms of church are not fully persuasive as ways of grappling with the challenges of post-Christendom, these challenges still need to be addressed. Perhaps engagement with emerging churches, cross-referenced with Anabaptist perspectives, might put such issues firmly on the agenda of inherited churches.

Mission initiatives

A critical issue in post-modern, post-Christendom society is how churches understand and practise mission. We cannot engage here with many questions that immediately arise about the scope and aims of such mission, appropriate methodology and diverse theological and ethical issues. But we will not appreciate the significance of the emerging church without recognising certain contemporary realities:

- Post-Christendom is a cross-cultural mission context, in which the Christian story is becoming unfamiliar and the church culturally alien. Inherited forms of evangelism, community involvement and socio-political action will not suffice.

- All churches, inherited and emerging, are required to embark on the journey to which the 1988 Lambeth conference called the Anglican Communion: from its inherited pastoral mode to 'a dynamic missionary emphasis'.

- In a plural society, diverse mission strategies will be needed for the church to find incarnational approaches to the cultures – de-churched and pre-churched, secular and religious, rich and poor, transient and settled, ethnic communities and sub-cultures – that today comprise Britain and other western societies.

Although not all emerging churches are mission-oriented, many have emerged as a response to this challenge in diverse mission contexts. Some are deliberate attempts to establish communities of faith in sectors of society where churches have been almost entirely absent. Others developed from creative community engagement or effective evangelistic activities, which were not initially intended to establish new churches.

Some emerging churches started in the late 1990s, when it was already apparent that the Decade of Evangelism had been far less effective than many had hoped and that planting more churches of the kind that already existed was hardly a sensible mission strategy. As Chapter 2 recognised, many involved in emerging churches do not regard themselves as church planters and react against this terminology, but many emerging churches developed (directly or indirectly) from the missiological and ecclesiological reflection in which church planters engaged during the late 1990s.

Emerging churches that are mission-oriented, then, may be responses to effective or ineffective mission:

- Some began as creative approaches to community engagement that were never intended to become churches but developed into churches as those involved found their ecclesiology radically affected by engagement with the community they were serving.

- Some emerged from evangelistic initiatives originally perceived as conduits through which new members might be added to existing churches. They grew into churches as those involved found the culture gap between new Christians and church too wide.

- Some were conceived as attempts to plant culturally-specific churches into particular places or networks, rather than hoping existing locations and styles of worship would attract those whom 1990s forms of evangelism and church planting had failed to reach.

Church leavers

Churches are emerging, not only to connect with people who are not and have never been involved in church, but to reconnect with those who have left church in recent years. Assessing the scale of disaffection from inherited churches (including New Churches) is difficult but a widely quoted figure of 1500 leaving every week indicates a haemorrhage that cannot be sustained if these churches are to survive.[29] This exodus is impacting all denominations and all kinds of churches – including new and growing churches and networks.

A new genre of books on this subject has emerged, based on sociological analysis, careful research and conversations with 'church leavers'. From these, tentative conclusions can be drawn:

- Inherited church is not working for significant numbers of Christians. Many have left in recent years and more will leave in the years ahead. Many others feel similarly about church but remain through loyalty, habit or inertia.

- Common complaints include autocratic leadership, inauthentic community, boring and uncreative worship, a sacred/secular dichotomy, disengagement with daily life and contemporary culture, unreflective dogmatism and failure to treat adults as adults.

- Leavers include deeply committed Christians, once at the heart of church and often in leadership roles. Churches are not losing people from the edges but from the centre. Many have been in church for years; leaving has been painful and often reluctant.

- Some leavers have abandoned their Christian faith; but many (perhaps over ninety per cent) have only abandoned church. Some leavers report significant growth in prayer, unprecedented liberty in sharing their faith with others (despite distaste for 'evangelism') and new enthusiasm for life since leaving church.

- Some leavers are uninterested in returning; others, despite everything, miss church and want to find a way back. Some are disillusioned and bitter, critical of church as an institution and not anticipating any change; others yearn for authentic church and are hoping something new might emerge.

- There is a significant mismatch between reasons given by leavers for leaving and explanations suggested by church leaders. The research highlights various issues, which include but is certainly not limited to reasons offered by church leaders.

We do not have space here to examine the reasons leavers give for leaving, but those with pastoral responsibility surely need to engage with this research, listen to leavers and ponder the implications for their churches.[30]

By no means all church leavers end up in emerging churches. Some eventually return to inherited churches, usually in a different tradition from the church they left. Many reject participation in any form of church, inherited or emerging, although how long living faith can be sustained in post-Christendom without some form of Christian community is as yet unclear. But a significant number of leavers do become involved in emerging churches, some of which have emerged as responses to this exodus from inherited church.

The concentration of leavers in some emerging churches raises questions. Can these churches deal effectively with the baggage leavers bring from churches they have left? Is there a danger of uniting around discontent rather than a positive vision? Is mission marginalised in reaction to forms of mission (especially evangelising) in inherited churches that many felt lacked integrity? Some are already leaving emerging churches, doubly disillusioned. But for many, emerging churches have enabled them to move beyond disaffection to a more authentic and liberating experience of church.

What do we mean by 'church'?

A question not yet addressed, which some readers may have been asking throughout these early chapters, is: what do we mean by 'church'? We may think we can answer this question fairly easily in relation to inherited church, although digging deeper may uncover various answers in a typical congregation. But the snapshots with which this chapter began and stories we will encounter in subsequent chapters pose challenges of definition. What are the essentials of church? What cannot be missing if we would label a community or activity 'church'?[31]

Several of us pondered this question in a conversation that eventually resulted in the launch of a website on which emerging church stories have been told and discussed.[32] What kinds of stories were we hoping for? Where were the boundaries? We pondered the need for theological boundaries and agreed *Trinitarian orthodoxy* was probably non-negotiable. We decided *catholicity* (or connectedness) was important if we were interested in churches that were ecumenical rather than isolationist in spirit.

We found helpful Robert Warren's diagram suggesting church was located at the intersection of three overlapping circles labelled *worship, mission* and *community*.[33] We were all aware of creative worship developments, innovative mission initiatives and sustaining community expressions embodying some but not all of these ecclesial dynamics. While we welcomed such activities, we were not sure about calling them 'church'. We were interested rather in stories with elements of worship, mission *and* community.

While we were not implying these characteristics – Trinitarian, catholicity, worship, mission and community – fully expressed our ecclesiology, they seemed a useful starting point in our engagement with emerging church. Which is all this very brief section represents – a starting point explaining why certain stories have or have not been included in this book. The question 'what is church?' underlies everything we are discussing and becomes the focus of most conferences I have addressed on the subject of emerging church.

Throughout the remainder of this book we will be probing more deeply into this question. For this is not just a question inherited churches are asking as they consider emerging churches; it is a question emerging churches are asking and reflecting back at the inherited church.[34] Perhaps conversations between inherited and emerging churches will help us answer this question in ways that connect with the mission context in which all churches now operate as well as being congruent with our founding story and two millennia of reflection on that story.

What do we mean by 'emerging'?

But if the characteristics we identified were not an attempt to define church comprehensively, nor were we suggesting all five must be fully present or perfectly balanced before we were interested in stories that were emerging. For 'emerging' is a dynamic concept, suggesting churches coming into being rather than fully formed.

This means, in practice, that the three intersecting circles may be different sizes and the starting point may be almost entirely in one circle.[35] Some stories may concern mission initiatives that have begun to embrace community and worship dimensions but where the mission dimension still predominates. Others may be expressions of worship or forms of community slowly developing mission perspectives and en route to becoming churches. Particularly in the early months, or even years, some groups may be so locally focused or culturally specific that connectedness is limited in practice, although catholicity of spirit may be evident.

Many stories told in the following chapters are of churches that are emerging, not yet mature or settled. Some groups will already be different from how they are described here. This is inevitable in any attempt to describe or interpret this fluid phenomenon. But we will feature groups that appear to be *on the way towards* exhibiting our five characteristics. This will mean excluding intriguing examples of creative mission, worship or community. It will mean making judgements that may be premature. But if the term 'emerging church' is to be useful, it cannot be stretched indefinitely.

There is one further point before proceeding. Contrasting 'emerging' and 'inherited' church is useful for the purpose of analysis but should not be regarded as entirely accurate or adequate. Actually, all churches are both inherited and emerging. Nobody starts with a blank canvas. The most radical church planting experiments or emerging church initiatives draw heavily on inherited ways of thinking about mission, worship and community. We all operate from within a tradition, however we critique and reshape what we have received. A sign of growing maturity in church plants is their renewed appreciation of traditions they overturned but now newly value.

Furthermore, even the most traditional inherited churches are emerging, for different people are involved in succeeding generations who shape the traditions in new ways, and no church is entirely unaffected by cultural changes happening around it. Indeed, unless we arrogantly claim our understanding and practice is perfect, we will always desire to continue emerging into churches that more adequately reflect the glory of Christ and embody the values and priorities of his kingdom.

So the stories will include churches planted from scratch and new developments from older churches. Some models can be found in more or less radical forms – some quite close to churches with which most readers will be familiar and others very different

41

from most inherited churches. Categorising and interpreting the emerging church and differentiating between inherited and emerging church is not an exact science.

Nor should we expect it to be if we accept Jesus' words about the Spirit's work in the Christian community: 'The wind blows wherever it pleases. You hear its sound, but you cannot tell where it comes from or where it is going. So it is with everyone born of the Spirit.'[36] Perhaps it would help if we used 'church' as a verb rather than a noun.

A very tentative classification

With this verse in our minds (and the caveats with which these chapters have been peppered), we turn finally to the question of classifying the emerging church.

Others have attempted this, usually with similar disclaimers. George Lings identifies four emerging church 'streams': those targeting networks rather than neighbourhoods; those expressing church through small groups; those changing the location, time and style of church; and those focusing on community development rather than worship services. But he recognises many churches mix different elements and approaches.[37]

Michael Moynagh proposes five categories: traditional church, rooted church, brand church, liquid church and workplace church. But he acknowledges some emerging churches are hybrids and gives many examples that do not fit neatly into these categories.[38] *Mission-shaped Church*, perhaps wisely, refrains from any attempt to categorise and simply offers an alphabetical listing of 'fresh expressions of church'.

My attempt, the result of many revisions, makes no claim to priority, nor do I expect it to be useful for long. In fact, rather than offering one way of classifying emerging churches, I am currently working with four models, each of which looks at emerging churches through a different lens and none of which tells the whole story.

Model 1
The simplest model distinguishes three kinds of 'emergence':

- Churches emerging *from* inherited church through a process of renewal and transformation. The outcome is not another church but church more or less radically different from the past in structure, ethos, style, focus or activities.

- Churches emerging *out of* inherited church through processes of community engagement, liturgical exploration, church planting or missional reflection. The outcome is a new (or embryonic) church that becomes more or less autonomous.

- Churches emerging *within* a particular context without the shaping influence of or significant connection to inherited church. The outcome is a new church, which may be more or less radical, that will need to build links with other churches.

Model 2
Another model identifies the 'orientation' or guiding factor in the emerging church:

- *Age-oriented*: churches designed to reach, sustain or be shaped by particular age groups.

- *Place-oriented*: churches operating in particular locations because of their mission potential, ambience or cultural fit.

- *Time-oriented*: churches functioning at particular times of the day or week that suit those who are already or may become involved.

- *Size-oriented*: churches that, reflecting on the implications of numbers for a church's ethos and purpose, opt for small-scale communities.

- *Culture-oriented*: churches rooted in particular ethnic or socio-economic groups, networks or sub-cultures.

- *Style-oriented*: churches exploring patterns of worship, models of leadership, rhythms of community life and other aspects of church.

- *Activity-oriented*: churches developing from the involvement of Christians in initiatives, projects and activities in the community.

- *Strategy-oriented*: churches configuring themselves in line with research into contemporary culture or determination of their core purpose.

Model 3

A third model identifies those with whom an emerging church is primarily concerned and for whom this church is planted or shaped:

- Church for the *pre-churched*: those with no prior experience of church, for whom church culture is alien and church language incomprehensible.

- Church for the *de-churched*: those who have some familiarity with inherited church but do not find such churches attractive or amenable.

- Church for the *semi-churched*: those who have some connection with existing churches and occasionally attend church activities but are not fully part of the church community.

- Church for the *post-churched*: those who have, for various reasons and often after years of involvement, decided to leave inherited churches.

- Church for the *anti-churched*: those with personal or ideological objections to church culture and maybe also to Christianity.

Using similar but not identical categories, *Mission-Shaped Church* reckons forty per cent of the population are non-churched, twenty per cent 'open de-churched', twenty per cent 'closed de-churched' and ten per cent 'fringe attenders'.[39] Significant problems with this terminology include its Christendom-oriented assumption that 'churched' is the cultural norm and its focus on church rather than Christian faith.

Model 4

The model we will mainly use[40] (cross-referencing with others) builds on the idea that three essential aspects of church are mission, community and worship.[41]

- Churches restructuring/reshaping for mission.

- Churches reconfiguring community.

- Churches re-imagining worship.

Emerging churches can be categorised in relation to the influence of these factors (in different combinations) on their emergence and development. Some are inspired by mission concerns, others by exploring fresh approaches to worship, others again by a search for authentic community. Many, of course, recognise that, whatever the initial focus, church involves all three aspects of mission, community and worship, and that transforming one aspect of church has implications for other aspects, even if these have not yet been fully explored.

It is worth stating again some limitations of these four models:

- By their nature these churches are 'emerging' so accurate classification is elusive and soon outdated.

- Many emerging churches are tentative and experimental, so classification may impose on them understandings they would not own.

- Those involved in emerging churches may be isolated, unaware of similar groups, so classification should not imply networks of churches.

- Many emerging churches cross over any categories that might be established, as eclecticism is a feature of emerging churches.

- Some emerging churches I know well could be allocated to three or more categories in some of the models.

It is probably safest, then, to regard this classification (whichever model is used) not as an accurate road map but as an artist's impression. We will use it as such in the following chapters.

4

Restructuring for Mission

Changing church or changing mission?

Those involved in emerging churches and those who reflect on
their significance draw lines around 'emerging church' in different places. Some are concerned primarily with emerging churches
that are very different from inherited church; others welcome
signs of renewal in inherited churches and the gradual emergence of churches more responsive to contextual factors. Some
are interested mainly in churches meeting in new locations; others
are hopeful about churches continuing to use familiar buildings
which develop new patterns of community.

Another factor in assessing churches – or even their inclusion in any classification of emerging church – is whether they
are motivated by and engaged in mission (however 'mission' is
defined).

Listening to some emerging church pioneers, it is evident that
what has emerged was not inspired or shaped by concerns for
the wider community. It has been nourishing and life-giving for
those involved, enabling existing Christians to explore new forms
of worship or more authentic patterns of community. But it was
not missional in its genesis and has not (yet) developed a sense
of mission beyond itself. This is the case in some, though not all,
alternative worship groups, where mission (and particularly evangelism) is suspect. Such groups would be wary of being bracketed
with emerging churches where mission is the driving force. Many
would resist using church planting terminology to describe their
emergence because of baggage associated with this.

For other practitioners and observers, however, mission is
the non-negotiable starting point. Their interest is restricted to
churches emerging from missiological reflection and engagement
with contemporary culture. They are either reluctant to describe
non-missional groups as 'emerging church', or they suspect
some emerging churches are self-indulgent distractions from the

mission to which all churches are called in post-Christendom. They are unimpressed by internal reconfiguration that does not impact the world beyond the church.

We have already explored the relationship between missiology and ecclesiology, but we need to mention this again, since we will be concentrating here (and in the next chapter) on emerging churches motivated and shaped by missional concerns. Some people involved in other emerging churches may regard these with disdain. Indeed, some may regard models included in this chapter as rooted in inherited church ethos and part of the problem! But, however we assess them, they are all attempts by Christians to discover forms of church that make sense in their diverse contexts. And the missional passion evident in many instances would not go amiss in apparently more edgy but sometimes missionally deficient emerging churches.

Restructuring churches for mission

Inherited church developed during the era when 'churchgoing' was normal and most families had some connection with churches (although this was less typical in urban communities). Mission, always peripheral to institutional maintenance, meant support for overseas missionaries, attempts to galvanise the faith of 'latent Christians' who comprised the bulk of the population and initiatives to improve society and care for needy individuals. Evangelicals and liberals debated the priority attached to different aspects of mission, but there was widespread agreement mission was something churches 'did', alongside other activities.

In post-Christendom, churches are becoming alien institutions telling a story few know or understand and (census returns notwithstanding) 'latent Christian' is an unhelpful concept. Many churches and denominations have embarked on journeys towards becoming truly missional. They realise it is insufficient to refine previous ways of 'doing' mission, add extra activities, or even locate mission higher up their agenda. A paradigm shift is required. Mission is not an item on the agenda – it is the agenda. Mission is not something churches plan or do but a divine initiative in which the church is invited to participate. Mission, not church, is the starting point.

Some churches have wisely resisted the temptation to 'bolt on' mission activities to an essentially maintenance-oriented institution, recognising this paradigm shift requires wholesale ecclesial restructuring. Attempts to implement this shift were underway in the early 1990s, before the current wave of emerging churches was discernible.

Three models attracted most attention: *seeker-oriented church, purpose-driven church* and *cell church*. All three are designed to ensure mission replaces maintenance as the driving force. They have common features but represent different approaches to restructuring churches for mission. Unlike many models we will encounter, hundreds of churches have adopted these approaches, some with track records of over a decade; dedicated organisations offer expertise and consultancy, and several books explicate the principles.

Seeker-oriented church

Seeker-oriented church was imported into Britain from the Willow Creek Community Church in Chicago, one of the fastest growing and highest profile American mega-churches, whose mission statement is: 'To turn irreligious people into fully devoted followers of Jesus Christ.' The church promotes a seven-step philosophy and strategy, emphasising relational evangelism, discovery of spiritual gifts, becoming disciples and service within and beyond the church.

The church's trademark feature is its 'service for seekers' – the Sunday service is a programme designed for 'unchurched' people. Careful research into the concerns and interests of 'unchurched Harry and Mary' determines its focus. Though not dissimilar from traditional 'guest services', seeker services are carefully choreographed, multi-media presentations, requiring intensive preparation. The themes are life-related and the arts and technology are used extensively. Visitors can be anonymous: there is no pressure to respond; the church expects seekers to visit many times before coming to faith. The church offers 'a safe environment for a dangerous message'. Those who respond are invited to midweek services for believers and other ministries the church runs.

Those who have observed or implemented this model have appreciated the value of a clear mission statement and thorough philosophy of ministry; the distinctiveness of a church that prioritises the 'unchurched'; the identification and knowledge of the target audience; the sensitivity to the feelings and aspirations of seekers; the commitment to excellence; and the emphasis on relational and patient evangelism.[42]

Some have expressed concerns: this market-driven approach offers a pre-packaged gospel to a culture highly suspicious of sales techniques; separating evangelism and worship may harm both; the gospel of the kingdom may be diluted, individualised or truncated; and focusing on seekers may hinder the development of full-orbed church, especially given the limited throughput from seeker services to other meetings.

How transferable is this model? It requires gifted leaders and performers, and very considerable investment of time and finance; the terminology is misleading – this is not 'church for the unchurched' as most who attend seeker services are semi-churched or de-churched; and it works mainly in middle-class settings with middle-aged people. As Eddie Gibbs comments: 'seeker-sensitive worship held in an auditorium devoid of religious symbols and led by polished, professional performers who are removed from the tattered and tawdry world of daily experience holds little appeal for many GenXers.'[43]

Attempts to develop seeker-oriented churches in Britain fall into two main categories: *seeker-targeted* and *seeker-sensitive*. More radical seeker-targeted churches embrace wholeheartedly the Willow Creek philosophy and strategy; seeker-sensitive churches incorporate elements of this model into inherited forms of church.[44]

Seeker-targeted churches have struggled to sustain this demanding approach to church and mission, especially given fairly limited responses in most situations. There are far fewer de-churched Britons; and pre-churched or anti-churched people are unlikely to respond to invitations. Few seeker-targeted churches have emerged.[45] However, being more seeker-sensitive has benefited many churches in their relationships with semi-churched and de-churched people.

Purpose-driven church
Purpose-driven church, which began to achieve in the mid-1990s the profile seeker-oriented church had attained in Britain earlier in the decade, is another import from the American mega-church

scene, this time the Saddleback Community Church in California. The principles on which it is founded will be familiar to anyone with a basic knowledge of 'church growth' literature from the 1970s and 1980s, although these are presented in a fresh and engaging way.[46]

The foundation of this model is a commitment to building church around five New Testament core purposes: worship, evangelism, fellowship, discipleship and ministry. This is implemented by means of a comprehensive strategy designed to draw people into church and encourage them to develop as disciples. Team leadership is needed in order to give balanced attention to all five purposes, and all decisions about staff, programmes, activities and finance are explicitly related to these core purposes. The church's mission is understood in relation to five concentric circles: the *community*, the *crowd*, the *congregation*, the *committed* and the *core*.

This highly organised and tightly focused form of church is often presented as being about church health rather than growth. Proponents claim it is adaptable to all cultural contexts, age groups and sizes of church, and that any tradition or denomination can apply the principles. There is clearly enormous value in identifying the core purposes of any organisation and ensuring its activities are related to these. Purpose-driven church challenges unfocused churches to review inherited activities and develop integrated strategies.

However, some question whether the five core purposes (explicitly based on Acts 2) adequately express the full purpose of the church of Jesus Christ (or even adequately exegete Acts 2); whether this model is culturally appropriate in contexts where less organisational approaches to community are favoured; whether the very conservative theology associated with it is helpful; whether any church should be 'driven', whatever its core purposes; and whether this approach is truly sustainable in smaller churches. There is considerable interest in some British churches in purpose-driven church and attempts to implement this approach, but none have been around long enough yet for a proper assessment.

Cell church
The 2003 Building Bridges of Hope consultation heard about an Anglican cell church in Kent – one of many to emerge in recent

years. Cell church, which since the mid-1990s has vied for attention with purpose-driven and seeker-oriented church, offers an alternative approach (intimate and participatory) to restructuring churches for mission, although based on similar principles. Enthusiasm for cell church is especially strong among Anglicans, Baptists and some New Church networks. Inspiration has come mainly from Faith Community Baptist Church in Singapore and the writings of Americans Ralph Neighbour, Bill Beckham and Carl George.

Cell churches are communities of Christians where the focus of church life is in small home-based groups, linked together within a larger structure. A working definition is a network of neighbourhood churches that meet as cells and unite for corporate celebrations. Cell church, then, has two components: *cell* and *celebration*. In some models, cell is primary; in others cell and celebration are given equal weight. (Some have a third level – *congregation* – but this may be a pastoral structure rather than an additional meeting.)

This bipartite arrangement is familiar in larger inherited churches with house groups and/or multiple congregations. What differentiates cell churches is the focus and activities of each level of church. Cells may be neighbourhood-based or network-based; have between eight and fifteen members; engage in relational evangelism; expect to grow in numbers and then divide; split to form new cells once they reach fifteen members; meet weekly and do everything inherited churches do – ministry, teaching, evangelism, communion, baptism and pastoral care. Cell *is* church, not a peripheral or secondary group, and cell membership is the top priority in church life.[47]

Four typical components of cell meetings are *welcome* (to incorporate newcomers), *worship* (usually participatory), *word* (learning together) and either *works* or *witness* (ministry to each other and evangelism). Each cell has a leader and apprentice leader, male or female, (so about one in five members of a cell church is a leader); their role is to guide the cells and encourage every-member ministry; every five cells have a supervisor and apprentice supervisor; every twenty-five cells have a pastor and apprentice pastor.

There are various models of cell church in Britain and different ways of initiating these:

- A few cell churches have been planted from scratch, starting with a single cell and multiplying from this base.

- Many more have emerged from inherited churches through 'transitioning', a process whereby they become fully-committed cell churches.

- Some have introduced a cell structure alongside inherited church, allowing members to participate in either model.

- The 'meta-church' model encourages churches to give equal weight to cells and celebrations rather than placing primary emphasis on cells.[48]

- Many inherited churches with home groups have incorporated cell church values into these groups.

Some advocates are dismissive of anything less than full-orbed cell church; others emphasise cell church values, rather than structure. Core values include: the centrality of Jesus, expectation that members will be growing and participating; development of honest, loving community life; and growth by multiplication.

Like seeker-oriented and purpose-driven church, cell church offers a clear focus, an orientation towards mission and a philosophy and structure encouraging commitment to core purposes. Unlike those models, it prioritises small groups and anticipates growth by multiplication rather than addition. Small groups are also vital in the other models but, as in inherited churches, these are ancillary to church as congregation.

Cell church is one expression of a widespread desire for human-scale community and relationships within churches that go beyond the superficial. We will encounter other examples. If the previous models offer anonymity in larger gatherings, cell churches offer groups where strangers can be known and included. Arguably, both approaches are needed to connect with different people in western culture.

Cell church has considerable potential for promoting community growth, developing leadership and other gifts, focusing on people rather than programmes and redressing the balance after centuries when inherited church has operated primarily through larger-scale gatherings. Cell church advocates use the image of a 'two-winged bird': in the Christendom era large-scale church was not balanced by small-scale church.

But some have encountered difficulties. This supposedly relational and empowering model can produce centralised, top-down and highly structured churches. The four components of cell meetings can become sacrosanct; group initiatives can be stymied by the need to hold cells together and focus on agreed purposes; and, despite wanting to major on people rather than programmes, the structure may require many meetings, especially for leaders. Problems also develop (as in other models) when structural changes are not rooted in deeply owned core values.

Furthermore, cell church is often accompanied by expectations of growth through restructuring churches for mission. But the model was adopted from less reserved cultures than Britain and contexts where rapid church growth was already occurring and cell structures enabled expanding churches to grow effectively. Expectations of rapid growth in British cell churches have rarely been realised.[49]

An interim assessment

Reflecting on these three attempts to restructure churches for mission, we might note the following:

- Unlike most examples of emerging church, these models have been around for several years in various locations, so there is experience available for churches drawn to them.

- There is considerable overlap between these models: purpose-driven churches may hold seeker services and make extensive use of cell groups.

- There is much common ground between these models in terms of the theology (evangelical/charismatic) that undergirds them, the white middle-class context within which they normally flourish and the mission-as-evangelism approach most adopt.

- Most examples of all three models have *emerged from* sizeable inherited churches (using terminology from the last chapter) rather than starting from scratch.

- Changing inherited church *structure* is demanding but achievable with time and effort; changing inherited church *mindset* takes longer and is not always achievable. Some attempts to restructure have foundered here.

- The few examples of introducing these models from scratch are not yet old enough to judge whether this offer greater potential than transitioning inherited churches.

- These models all operate with the inherited 'come to us' approach to mission and seem likely to connect primarily with the de-churched and semi-churched (who comprise a shrinking proportion of contemporary society).

- All three models were adopted from contexts where Christendom is alive and well or churches are growing rapidly. Attempts to implement them in Britain (where few would regard themselves as seekers or be particularly interested in attending either cells or services) have resulted in considerable disappointment in many places as comparable results have not been forthcoming.

- Many emerging churches would interpret these models as modern rather than post-modern (despite claims that cell church works well in a culture that prefers small-scale and grass-roots structures), desperate attempts to recalibrate old models rather than pointers to the future.

- From an Anabaptist perspective, cell church has most to offer. It challenges clericalism, is Christocentric and promotes multi-voiced church life. Although still too often top-down rather than bottom-up, it has the potential to transform institutional church into more organic, domestic and relational community.

- Viewed through a post-Christendom lens, cell church also seems the most appropriate for developing a marginal missionary movement free from the infrastructure of a fading era and declining church.

Inherited churches (especially from traditions other than those from which seeker-oriented, purpose-driven and cell churches have emerged) may find aspects of these models uncongenial, but they raise important issues and challenges:

- To what extent are inherited churches working towards an agreed purpose that precludes activism or lethargy?

- What would it mean for inherited church to reconfigure itself as a 'church for others' prioritising those beyond the congregation?

- What role do small groups (by whatever name) play in inherited churches and their growth in discipleship and community?[50]

- How strong is the element of evangelism within what inherited churches may claim is their holistic understanding of mission?[51]

G12 cell church

An alternative cell church structure, pioneered by a large charismatic church in Bogotá, Colombia, is the G12 model, which several British churches have adopted. The 2003 Building Bridges of Hope consultation heard from a church in Liverpool that is in the early stages of implementing this approach. Although this shares many assumptions and values of 'traditional' cell church, there are significant differences in structure and ethos.

The G12 model develops through establishing groups of twelve people, each of whom forms their own further group of twelve, laying a foundation for exponential growth rather than cells dividing into two. Unlike other cell churches, where division means (in a growing church) everyone experiences frequent changes of cell membership, in the G12 model everyone belongs to a permanent group of twelve as well as leading their own 'open group'. Another feature of this model is that cells are homogeneous, with groups for men, women, young people and children. The expectation that each person can develop their own group requires an even higher commitment to multiple leadership than in other cell churches. An ongoing 'school of leaders' trains emerging leaders.

G12 does not, as sometimes assumed, mean 'group of twelve' but 'government of twelve': advocates argue this model is based on a biblical and spiritual principle. Consequently, despite being presented as a decentralised approach that affirms the leadership potential of every Christian, the model is hierarchical and the structural arrangements are often regarded as non-negotiable, impervious to contextual factors. There is strong ideological commitment to setting growth goals, a centrally planned discipling process and a fixed agenda concentrating on typical evangelical/charismatic concerns. But proponents contrast its relational leadership style with the managerial style (through zones and districts) of other cell churches.[52]

Attempts to implement this model in British churches are still in their early stages, so any assessment, as usual with emerging churches, must be provisional. The question already being asked (in addition to those raised above) is whether this Colombian model can be transferred into post-Christendom western culture, especially given the reluctance to contextualise it. Can it thrive, or even survive, in a context where rapid numerical growth is very unusual and there will be stronger cultural resistance than in Bogotá to such a highly structured and homogeneous model?

An unusual application of G12 is envisaged by an emerging church operating under the *Cutting Edge* initiative.[53] With a very different ethos and spirituality from other G12 initiatives, *Contemplative Fire* envisages the proliferation of cells through 'contemplative evangelism'.

Its founder writes: 'A personal and corporate outworking of Trinitarian theology, together with a commitment not only to spiritual formation but also to religious formation within the context of the biblical tradition and the liturgical year, will provide the dynamic framework for the emergence and seeding of new Christian communities.'

Contemplative Fire 'draws substantially from the threefold dynamic of prayer, study and action as expressed in the New Testament and in the finest examples from the monastic movement and Christian mission over the centuries.'[54]

Minsters and Clusters

A different approach to restructuring for mission is the recognition of some churches as minsters and the development of clusters. Once again, these models presuppose a large-church starting point.

Ian Bradley proposes the creation of new *minsters* (reworking historic examples) as an alternative to increasingly desperate efforts to maintain a parish system already in trouble and soon to be stretched beyond breaking point.[55] Large minster churches with multiple staff, skills and resources can be recognised as 'resource churches' with missional responsibility for areas larger than parishes and as centres of support, training and strategic co-ordination for nearby smaller churches. If some inherited denominational structures become non-viable in the next thirty years, as their own projections predict, minsters may be vital for developing strategic mission initiatives.

This will require renegotiation of relationships between many large churches and their smaller neighbours. Potential minsters may have a reputation for being absorbed in their own activities and uninterested in the fortunes of other local churches. They may also be perceived (rightly or wrongly) as hindering the growth of other churches, by attracting Christians who might otherwise join more local congregations. Some large churches grow primarily through transfer of existing Christians rather than conversion growth. On the other hand, small churches may be jealous of their larger neighbours, threatened by their success, unwilling to invite or receive help and inaccurate in their assessment of attitudes within larger churches.

Some churches are already, in effect, operating as minsters.[56] Perhaps the best-known example (although this terminology is not used) is Holy Trinity, Brompton, which has not only planted several churches across London but is the home of the *Alpha* course and other resources that are appreciated nationally and internationally.[57] Needless to say, this appreciation is counterbalanced by the sense of threat some London churches feel from their huge neighbour. The corporate vision the Assemblies of God adopted in 1997 included a commitment to establishing 'resource churches'.

The development of *clusters* may or may not be associated with minsters but also represents a restructuring of large churches. If large churches are to move beyond holding celebrations and running centralised programmes, they need to subdivide into more manageable units. Cell church is one option, but their limited size and domestic setting may be inappropriate for some forms of mission. We will also encounter a multi-congregational model, where different expressions of church develop within the same ecclesial framework (often on the same premises). But multiple congregations generally require all aspects of church to operate within each congregation, albeit linked together as one church.

Clusters are more flexible and mission-focused than multiple congregations, but larger and less homogeneous than cells.

Clusters represent an attempt to rediscover congregation-sized communities that need not be autonomous or carry the weight of being fully-fledged churches. They have a clear focus, around which cluster members gather, while the involvement of these members in celebrations and cells offer both a broader experience of church and greater intimacy.

St Thomas Crookes, Sheffield has developed clusters. The church's website explains:

'Cluster allows us to do certain things that are not possible in either the small group or the celebration. Clusters provide a greater context for encouraging every-member ministry than small group alone. In particular, they provide the bridge between these two other groups that allows members to grow in their giftings and ministry . . . Clusters also provide the structure for church growth through mission across the whole city, not only by raising up leaders but also by increasing the "surface area" – through which people can enter – of the church.

'Clusters meet in several areas of the city . . . and in a wide variety of venues – schools, community centres, café bars, restaurants, pubs, a museum, and a double garage, to name a few! Location is defined by the primary mission focus of the cluster: a cluster aiming to reach a suburban neighbourhood might meet in the local school; another reaching a more deprived neighbourhood in the function room of a pub...'[58]

A concern about this model is whether a three-tier approach (cell, cluster, celebration) is sustainable. There is not simply a question of proliferating meetings, which careful planning can resolve, but the issue of whether members can feel part of three different levels of church. However, if the focus and purpose of each level is distinct, this may be less problematic.

This approach may indicate congregation-sized church is not defunct. The suggestion that this will be squeezed out between intimate small-scale and celebratory large-scale churches has worried not only members of medium-sized congregations but observers who are not persuaded that either small-scale or large-scale church is fully adequate. Clusters may be one of several indications that congregational models still have value, although this suggestion should not be interpreted as unambiguous endorsement of the status quo in many congregations.[59]

Café-style church

Restructuring of a more practical kind is required for the final model in this chapter. Café-style church involves churches setting out their normal meeting place in café format, [60] with groups of chairs around small tables. Most café-style churches have a similar philosophy to seeker-oriented churches.

Café-style church may happen monthly, or less frequently, as special events designed to be more seeker-friendly than services with traditional seating arrangements. Coffee and doughnuts may be served; newspapers, cold drinks and nibbles may be available. The format may be either more interactive or more presentational than usual, but the hope is that this and the atmosphere will be welcoming to visitors. There are examples of café-style churches that always meet like this.

A former student planted a café-style church that never meets in any other format. He told me:

'The idea appealed for several reasons. Our culture is less formal and more leisure-orientated, informal eating out is now the cultural norm, wine bars are common and if our weather was more suited we would have a bigger street café scene. In any event many people have sampled the continental experience and are familiar with taverna style life. Eating out is what we do with friends, and since friendship evangelism is our best way forward at present, it provides a low-risk frame-work for people to invite friends to church.

'Meeting in a school dining hall we had a ready supply of tables and chairs which made logistics easy. We placed four or five chairs in horseshoe style around tables. Our theory was that it would be less threatening to strangers to sit around tables in small groups than feel imprisoned in a row with no means of escape. Since we also established an informal environment, folk felt free to get up and move around at any time.

'Tea, coffee, biscuits, plus fresh fruit and squash for the children were served in the first 15 minutes and taken to

> the tables. We would then gently transition to informal worship. We split the time into short "sound/vision bites" that were multimedia based. We would typically include drama or video, taped music, testimony, poetry etc., to illustrate the topical life-related theme. The "sermon" would be one or two 10-minute maximum explanations of how the Bible is relevant today. We agonised about whether to include sung worship but eventually did on the basis that, as we had a "cabaret" style format, music was appropriate.'[61]

Although café-style church hardly represents radical restructuring, practitioners have been surprised by its impact and the changed atmosphere and ethos that results from moving furniture around and introducing more relaxed elements into meetings. As many emerging churches have found, architecture, lay-out, ambience, seating and other physical aspects are more significant than many had previously realised. Simply changing the location of tables and chairs can stimulate fresh thinking about the kind of community church is and can be more welcoming for those who are unfamiliar with church.

As we proceed to investigate emerging churches that appear more radical, perhaps we should not too quickly dismiss the restructuring of inherited church represented by models in this chapter. Some may not only appear more attainable to many people in inherited churches but may result in churches changing in unexpected ways when they embark on what seems to be only limited restructuring. However, a limitation of these models is the inbuilt expectation that they will encourage people to 'come to church'. As such, they are unlikely to reach beyond the diminishing fringe of de-churched and semi-churched people in our society.

5

Reshaping for Mission

Restructuring churches for mission whilst continuing to rely on a *centripetal* approach that expects 'seekers' to attend services in church buildings is inadequate. In post-Christendom, where interest in spirituality does not readily translate into churchgoing, a *centrifugal* approach is needed. We must 'go' to people instead of hoping they will 'come'. Missionaries into western culture will be the 'seekers'!

Importing church into different places

Some emerging churches are responding to this challenge by importing church into places that are culturally more congenial than church buildings. This is not entirely new, for many church planters have used community centres, schools, snooker halls, shops and other venues. But these locations did not usually shape the churches they planted, except superficially. Many church planters in the 1990s attempted to take church *geographically* closer to people, but some emerging churches are trying to take church *culturally* closer to people.

Workplace church

Many Christians meet with work colleagues for prayer, Bible study, mutual support or to discuss issues of common interest. City-centre churches have developed lunchtime services for business people or provided quiet space for reflection during the day. But such activities are generally seen as adjuncts to church, not church. These people are expected to belong to neighbourhood churches where they live.

Four factors have challenged this expectation and encouraged an alternative strategy. First, long working hours and increased commuting time have made participation in neighbourhood churches hard to sustain, especially if midweek evening activities are required. Second, research evidence indicates that many people have more in common with work colleagues than neighbours,[62] so faith-sharing is probably more effective at work. Third, for many (though not all) people work is more engaging and fulfilling than in past generations, offering a sense of vocation once exercised through church activities. Fourth, many churches offer little to members in relation to discipleship at work (a frequent complaint of church leavers).[63]

Some Christians still participate in neighbourhood churches, but their relationships with Christians at work seem more authentic expressions of 'church' than their experience on Sundays or as they collapse exhausted into home groups. Others no longer belong to such groups and regard workplace church as their main Christian community. Some workplace churches have emerged spontaneously; others are being established deliberately to respond to the opportunities and demands of contemporary work patterns. Some cell churches have workplace-based cells or cells comprising (and reaching out to) those working in similar jobs or professions. Some churches with clusters have workplace clusters. In a recent issue of *Encounters on the Edge* George Lings reports and reflects on a number of workplace church initiatives.[64] An industrial chaplain mentioned to me a church emerging among civil servants and another in a bus company.

St Peter's is an Anglican church with an unusual location and parish. It is a 140-foot barge with a capacity of 100 moored in West India Dock, near Canary Wharf in East London's Docklands.

Located within the parish of St Anne's, Limehouse, its own parish is not the local neighbourhood but the thousands who work in Canary Wharf.

St Peter's offers Wednesday lunchtime teaching events, prayer for forty-five minutes at 7.45 on Tuesday mornings and a Thursday lunchtime discipleship course.

Questions about workplace church include:

- Is it unhealthily homogeneous and too narrowly focused?
- Can it be practised without alienating other work colleagues or intruding on work commitments?

- What is the impact on families no longer worshipping together?
- How sustainable is workplace church, and does this matter?

Pub church

Another community focus, and somewhere people are relaxed, is the pub. Indeed, many have commented that pub culture at its best offers the warm, accepting environment some churches lack – and that the regulars demonstrate a commitment for which many churches yearn!

Can church be imported into pubs as another expression of going where people feel comfortable, rather than trying to entice them into church buildings where many feel uncomfortable? Several forms of pub church have emerged. Some simply hire a room and hold services similar to those normally held in church buildings. Others organise special events designed to entertain and challenge those who participate. Others have become more integrated into the pub community and run open events which regulars accept as part of pub life. Here are two Welsh examples:

Zac's Place – 'a church for ragamuffins' – started in Swansea in 1998. According to its website,[65] this 'came about as a direct result of requests from bikers and musicians we were ministering among who wanted to know more, but could see little relevance of main-stream church. It continues to be specifically for those who would not normally feel comfortable in traditional church settings and also for those on the fringes of, or dropped out of, church for what ever reason.

'The Sunday night pub gatherings aim to provide oppor-tunity for expression of and enquiry into the Christian faith in a relaxed pub environment. The format consists of quality live music and other performance art and straight talking in languages and images that relate at street level.'

In 2003 the church obtained city-centre premises to develop additional community initiatives, but it contin-ues to operate as a pub church.

Bar None is based in Cardiff. Its website gives a rationale for pub church:

'For the first Christians, recorded in the New Testament, the actual time or place of getting together didn't matter. To them no building was sacred – just a space to be used. Jesus had said before he left that whenever two or three gathered in his name he would be there. People would eat and drink, both socially and as a symbol (sometimes called the Lord's Supper or Communion), they would worship God and tell stories about Jesus. As a marginalised and persecuted group they had to depend on each other for everything – possessions were shared and the weak were protected by the stronger. It was a genuine community. It was church.

'Our aim at *Bar None* is to plant ourselves back in the heart of a community, to bar none that are looking for answers or a place to ask questions. Pubs by definition are public space, they feel inhabitable and unpretentious, a quality that, unfortunately, is not shared by many churches.'[66]

But are these evangelistic activities or church?[67] Those involved say they are churches. *Bar None*'s website, introducing midweek groups for those who want to go deeper, insists: 'Our primary aim is to be church, to be a community, rather than being an evangelistic tool.'

Club-culture church

A variant on pub church is the attempt in several British cities to import church into city-centre clubs. Just as some identify more strongly with work colleagues than neighbours, others feel greater affinity with those who share their love of dance, music and club culture than those they either work with or live near. In a networked society, incarnational mission will mean importing church into network communities as well as neighbourhood communities.[68]

Some club-culture churches operate physically in the club environment, meeting in city-centre clubs, pubs and wine bars. Their members participate actively in the club scene, building relationships and inviting friends to church activities. Others have developed their own venues to host events that resonate with those who feel at home in club culture.[69] Here are two Scottish examples:

The Crypt is part of Queen's Park Baptist Church, Glasgow. Run in partnership with the music and mission group *ngm*,[70] this is 'church for a new generation of young people who want to experience God within a setting that represents their culture.'[71]

The Crypt is a purpose-built youth venue in the basement of the church building, containing a 10^2m dance floor, stage area, DJ booth, lighting and video systems, two pool tables, an air hockey table, computer consoles, arcade machines, table tennis table, tuck shop and eight large seating booths.

Peter Neilson tells the story of 'Exploring Church for Club Culture', an initiative resulting from a parish survey, which revealed that 2000 people lived in it, 8-10,000 worked in it and 20,000 arrived at night and at weekends for entertainment, mainly clubbing.[72] This initiative revolved around three centres of activity:

Urban Soul: an 'attempt to express worship in the culture of the club world.'

Soulspace: 'an attempt to do three things: connect with the rages and dreams of urban young people, work alongside them to create music which is the life blood of the club scene, and to offer a safe space to explore pain – our own or the pain of the world.'

EH1: 'a cafe where clubbers meet when they wake up from Saturday evening. EH1 is where it all began and where it all connects. Over two years the team have been there, meeting people and building friendships. This is the junction box: as *Urban Soul* and *Soulspace* relate to widely different groups of people, EH1 provides the relational bridge.'

More recently this initiative has evolved into a small community called *Raven*.[73]

Café church

Café churches have flourished in Australia, where climate and culture are conducive to churches operating in cafés. Café church there usually means Christians meeting in a café and engaging with people for whom this is a natural and familiar meeting-place. The focus may be on post-churched or pre-churched people; there is often a strong emphasis on the arts and alternative worship; and the café may or may not be run by Christians.

'*Cafechurch* (at the Universal Café in Melbourne) is about a group of Christians who want to enjoy church and each other through the challenge of community. We meet weekly in a café where we share our faith in a forum that is informal and interactive . . .

'Basically we are a growing community on a journey towards Christ, endeavouring to love God and to love people with all that we have. We frequently gather informally in a café, where we are able to share our journey of faith . . .

'Here is a list of the sort things we value: God (worship, obedience, trust); community (honesty, acceptance authenticity, openness, friendship); intentional discipleship (commitment, accountability, love); mission (outward expression of service); our cultural expression (creativity, diversity, relevance).'[74]

Café churches are emerging in Britain, although *café-style churches* (considered in Chapter 4) are more common. Michael Frost and Alan Hirsch describe monthly events in the Medicine Bar café in Birmingham when a 'spiritual space' (*Maji*) is created and local artists and others explore faith.[75] *Mission-shaped Church* tells the story of *Rubik's Café*,[76] which has emerged from an initiative in Bristol club culture. The story of Swansea's *Red Café* appears on the emergingchurch.info website.[77] And some pub churches are considering running café churches alongside their pub-based activities.

Some features of pub churches, café churches and club-culture churches highlight issues for inherited church:

- The use of ambient music, contemporary dance music and performance artists, rather than congregational singing.

- The provision of 'safe spaces' in which issues of faith and life can be explored in an open, non-judgemental environment.

- Participation depends on relationships and shared culture rather than living in geographical proximity.

- Any imbalance between genders may be towards men rather than women.

Enterprise church

In *The Shaping of Things to Come*, Frost and Hirsch applaud churches operating in 'incarnational mission mode', rather than 'attractional, dualistic and hierarchical Christendom-mode', and exhibiting four characteristics: 'proximity spaces, shared projects, commercial enterprise and emerging indigenous faith communities.'[78]

They give two English examples, both of which also appear in *Changing Churches*,[79] and others from America and their own nation, Australia. They argue that Christians should build relationships through sharing in projects and enterprises, rather than trying to persuade people to participate in church activities. These relationships are the context, not only for faith-sharing,[80] but for the emergence of indigenous faith communities, rooted in local culture rather than imposed from outside.

The mindset-shift involved in this understanding of how churches emerge is huge. In the past such activities were seen as bridges into 'proper church', but increasingly in post-Christendom the cultural gap cannot be bridged. Groups are emerging in various places that cannot be perceived as bridges into inherited church: they are becoming church in diverse contexts. At a conference in February 2004, one participant reported a church emerging from a ballet school; another mentioned a church emerging from an urban bread-making venture. A recent *Encounters on the Edge* booklet considers whether *A Rocha* communities might be emerging churches.[81]

Enterprises involving the arts and social justice are becoming sufficiently numerous almost to require an additional category in this classification of emerging churches. Not all are yet self-consciously churches, but the dynamics of spiritual community are often present, at least in embryonic form. *Urban Space* in Wakefield and *Intermission* in London are examples.[82]

Sometimes the intention from the outset is for a church to emerge from an enterprise. Sometimes this is a last resort, as this comment from someone considering planting a church in a football club indicates: 'we are interested in forms of alternative church, because no matter what we have tried over the years it has proved extremely hard to get the players into a conventional church.' Such comments and initiatives challenge inherited churches to recognise the cultural gulf between them and the surrounding culture. If they do not welcome the emerging churches described here, how will they bridge this gap?

Cyber-church

Importing church into different places goes beyond physical locations. If pubs, clubs and workplaces are centres of community, so is the internet. Incarnation may usually mean flesh-and-blood faith communities, but can it be applied to virtual communities fostered via websites, email, blogging and chat rooms?

Some have suggested internet chat rooms are equivalent to the markets of the ancient world, in which early missionaries shared their faith. Cyber-evangelism has been with us for some time, ranging (like other forms of evangelism) from predictable and gross to creative and subtle examples. A leading British site is the ecumenically supported and impressive <www.rejesus.co.uk>.

Numerous churches and organisations use websites to provide teaching, training and resources, offering sermons, articles and songs in downloadable format, networking members of dispersed communities, distributing daily devotional material by email, leading people through on-line labyrinths, and much else.[83]

But cyber-church goes beyond using the internet as a communication tool. Various groups are exploring forming web-based congregations, with or without physical gathering places. Some use the internet to build and sustain faith communities but encourage members also to meet face to face. Others dispense entirely with physical community and connect only through the internet.[84]

The *Cutting Edge* initiative is supporting *I-church*, an attempt to create a diocesan web-based church. Its remit is:

'To provide a focus of Christian community for those who wish to explore Christian discipleship but who are not able, or do not wish, to be participant members of a local congregation.

'To provide an additional means of support to those who do not find all that they need within their own worshipping community.

'To provide continuing connectivity with Christians who travel, either through their work or in their life-style, and who are not able to maintain relationships with a geographical Christian community.

'The spirituality of the community will be based on that of one of the religious communities of the Diocese, reflecting a commitment to prayer, study and social action . . . Online daily worship according to the new Common Worship, or some similar liturgical provi-sion, together with reading for the day, and a section for prayer requests from community members forms a central part of the web site.

'Visitors are welcome to I-church in the same way that they are to any physical church. They can read the posts, and are welcome to any of the meetings or events . . . One of the key purposes of I-church is to provide a community for those who do not find participant membership of a local church easy, and it will therefore reflect an inclusive attitude to Christian faith and disci-pleship.

'I-church is different from a local congregation. Although I-church will provide the opportunity for meeting, there is no obligation on members to meet together. Some may wish to meet others from the same geographical area, or to pursue a particular task, or to learn about Christian spirituality and discipleship in a variety of ways. Others may find that I-church meets their needs without any physical meeting.'[85]

The above categories are indicative of contexts into which church is being imported. They offer encouraging evidence of missional creativity and courage but raise many questions, especially about the nature of Christian community, for those involved and those watching with interest.

Incarnating church into different cultures

Importing church into different places often involves changes in style and ethos as well as location. Engaging in mission among those who participate in city-centre club culture requires culturally attuned as well as appropriately located churches. Cultural attunement is a feature of other emerging churches whose raison d'être is to incarnate the gospel into the many cultures and sub-cultures of post-modern western society.

Across Britain inherited church notice boards proclaim 'All Welcome'. This implies a commitment to all sectors of the community and the desire to be inclusive. However, despite good intentions, in reality congregations are often homogeneous in age, class, ethnicity and culture, failing to engage effectively with a diverse community beyond the congregation. All are welcome, but many do not feel welcome. All are welcome, but they must conform to inherited church culture. There are many groups in society separated from most churches by a cultural gap seemingly too wide to cross from either side.

Some emerging churches have concluded it is as unrealistic to expect inherited church to embrace all the sub-cultures in a community as it is to ask those who are culturally distant from inherited church to leap this gap. A different approach is to start churches that incarnate the gospel into these networks and sub-cultures. What emerges may be more homogeneous than many inherited churches, but it will be a different expression of homogeneity making a distinctive contribution to the heterogeneity of the church in the locality.

Network church

We have already used 'network' terminology to differentiate from neighbourhood churches emerging churches that operate within relational networks. These may or may not meet in different places from neighbourhood churches; their distinguishing feature is that their constituency is defined demographically, not geographically. What members have in common is not where they live but who they know and why they know them. Network churches, recognising the networked nature of contemporary society, are attempting to incarnate gospel and church into these networks, rather than expecting people to join churches in neighbourhoods where they do little but sleep.

Common factors in networks might be membership of a gym, support for a football club, patronage of a club or wine bar, passion for a pastime, enjoyment of the same music, a particular dress code, commitment to social justice, employment in a line of business or other expressions of shared identity. Network churches are as ready to operate within such networks as early missionaries were to use Jewish relational networks in predominantly Gentile cities.

Network churches may be similar to inherited churches in how they worship, the kinds of buildings they use or the activities they organise. But their understanding of community and their focus for mission is quite different. Network churches are not all homogeneous, since those with shared interests in one sphere of life may be diverse in other ways. But the incarnational principle provokes questions about where and when these churches meet, how they are structured and what forms of church resonate with the culture and interests of those involved. Aware that faith-sharing is most authentic and effective in the context of relationships, their evangelism is along network lines rather than within geographical areas where they know few people. Two of the better known examples are *The Net* in Huddersfield and *B1* in Birmingham.[86]

The Building Bridge of Hope consultation in 2002 heard the story of *DNA* ('Dynamic New Anglian Networks') in Colchester. Its expressed aim was to develop a network of worshipping communities linked with 'mission units'.

At that time there were four mission units – among international students, young adults (sixteen to nineteen), workers and families with young children.

The philosophy undergirding this emerging church is an attempt to form units that are not congregations but are devoted to mission, with the expectation that their mission will shape the congregation to which they relate.[87]

Culture-specific church

But some network churches are more homogeneous and culturally very different from inherited churches. The question asked by some radical and creative missionaries into contemporary western societies is what church might look like if it takes root within sub-cultures and develops in culturally specific forms. The motivation is both to plug gaps in the church's mission in post-modern culture and to encourage indigenous faith communities to emerge. An emerging church leader in Florida explained to me that he and his colleagues are working 'to develop and plant home churches into the mission gaps of our city . . . These small expressions of church serve to bring the church into the neigh-bourhoods and networks that are unreached with the gospel. We call these niches "gaps".'

In London, Manchester and elsewhere churches are emerging among Goths, whose physical appearance, musical preferences and dress code would be distinctive in inherited churches (and many emerging churches). This is a sub-culture with its own values and ethos, as well as shared cultural norms, which operates along network lines. Emerging Goth churches are attempting to cross-pollinate Goth values and gospel values.[88]

An Australian church planter, a member of a cross-cultural mission agency and linked with a programme committed to training leaders for mission in post-modern culture, is attempting to plant a church into the science fiction community in his city. How else do churches connect with this sub-culture? What will this church look like? When and where will it meet? In what ways will it engage with the passions of this commu-nity? How will it relate to other churches?

Some are advocating 'messianic mosques' as an alterna-tive to traditional approaches to establishing churches in Muslim communities. Just as 'messianic synagogues' aim to incarnate the gospel in ecclesial forms that value participants' Jewish heritage, so messianic mosques retain much Muslim culture and religious practice, rather than requiring participants to adopt alien cultural norms, but acknowledge Jesus as the Son of God rather than just a great prophet.[89]

Youth church

The alienation of teenagers and young adults from inherited church is widely known and it has become evident that New Churches are also struggling to retain their own young people and connect effectively with others. Churches and youth organisations have responded by establishing youth congregations (by 2000 at least 100 may have been established).⁹⁰ Most relate to inherited churches rather than being autonomous, but these are much more than youth events. They may operate as regional celebrations or weekly congregations and usually have cell-based pastoral systems.

Youth churches focus initially on participants within a defined age range. They may be neighbourhood-based or network-based, although typically relationships develop along network lines. Youth culture is, of course, subdivided in many ways, so no one expression even of youth church can connect culturally with all young people. But youth church (some prefer 'youth culture church') attempts to incarnate the gospel in ecclesial forms that relate to young people. It is also about empowerment: emerging churches shaped and led by young people themselves.

Such developments raise questions and concerns:

- In societies which both idolise and exploit youth culture, can youth churches avoid being co-opted by cultural forces and contributing to increased inter-generational alienation?

- What happens when people reach the upper age limit of youth churches – does the age limit stretch or do they transfer into other churches?

- If it stretches so youth church gradually embraces young adults, then thirty-somethings, then middle-aged members, will new youth churches be started every few years?

- If it does not stretch, to what will members graduate? I have had conversations with two women in their early twenties too old for youth church and feeling bereft. One answer is emerging young adult or GenX churches.⁹¹ But will this create a stratified church community?

However, the missional significance of youth churches is not just related to the age of participants: young people represent emerging culture, with which all churches must engage. Graham Cray writes: 'it is the changing cultural and therefore missiological context which has led to the development of youth congregations. Some may well prove to be temporary measures until the wider church develops better habits in welcoming and empowering the young. But to plant the church in an emerging cultural era has to begin with the young. Some of these experiments may pioneer ways of being church that will be multigenerational and the mainstream in a few decades time.'[92]

Children's church

If inherited churches are struggling with teenagers, they are facing a huge challenge in relation to children, whose disconnection from church during the past thirty years provides dramatic evidence of church decline and the end of Christendom. Excluding the influence of church schools, only ten to fifteen per cent of children now have any contact with churches and only four per cent attend Sunday School or its equivalent. Perhaps two-fifths of churches have no children's work.[93] Traditional approaches are simply not working. A generation of children is growing up which does not know the Christian story at all.

Some have developed expressions of church designed for children, rather than trying to integrate them into churches designed primarily for adults. Most are churches run by adults for children but, as with youth churches, some attempt to empower children to help shape church. The format may be modelled on the rather manic culture of Saturday morning television, with fast-moving, noisy and energetic activities and worship, prayer and teaching interspersing games and competitions. The venue may be a school, church hall, community centre or the back of a lorry in a park.

Thus far such initiatives sound like the special children's weeks many churches run in school holidays – although running such programmes consistently throughout the year requires considerable commitment and creativity. But the most impressive children's churches are those which involve a committed group of adults not only running these events but visiting *every child* in their home *every week*. The double outcome of such visiting is strong relationships built with whole families and children developing real friendships with adult mentors.[94]

Some will grieve the development of children's churches, doubt the wisdom of this strategy and the sustainability of such churches, and yearn for truly intergenerational communities. But children's church raises questions about the marginalisation of children in many churches, the dissatisfaction many experience with so-called all-age services and the limited alternative responses to the absence of children from inherited churches. It may also challenge us to revisit the incident where Jesus placed a child among his disciples and urged them to humble themselves like children and welcome children in his name as those who are great in the kingdom of heaven.[95] Avoiding sentimentality, we might ask what our churches would be like if children were at the centre.

Culture-specific and age-specific churches provoke concern or outrage from those who perceive them as illegitimate and deeply regrettable for several reasons:

- Such churches offer a narrow range of relationships and deprive members of opportunities for growth in discipleship through relating to people different from them.

- Such churches fly in the face of the breaking down of barriers at the heart of the gospel of reconciliation the church proclaims.

- Such churches in societies wracked by ethnic and intergenerational conflict risk exacerbating rather than addressing problems.

- Such churches do not square with the mixed congregations we read about in the New Testament or with its eschatological vision of redeemed humanity.

These are theological, ethical and pastoral issues that cannot be dismissed or quickly resolved. But they are not issues emerging churches are unaware of or insensitive to. One response is to differentiate between targeted mission strategies and longer-term discipleship strategies that involve forging relationships between culture-specific or age-specific churches and different churches. Another less charitable but legitimate response is to suggest such criticisms apply equally to many homogeneous inherited churches. Though these may be homogeneous by default rather than design, the challenge remains. Inherited churches that disapprove of niche churches for neglected sub-cultures face the challenge of finding alternative strategies to engage with people beyond their own comfort zones.

Church for marginalised groups

If children in church and society are variously pampered, patronised and marginalised (sometimes all at the same time), other groups are in danger of being marginalised by the churches as well as society. 'All welcome' may be our official position, but some people may be more welcome than others.

There are various reasons for such conscious or unconscious marginalising of people who threaten the security, comfort, ethical sensitivities or cultural norms of inherited church. From the late 1950s, personal and institutional racism has been one factor in the emergence of Caribbean and other ethnic churches (which we will investigate in Chapter 7). A mixture of fear and ethical principle has resulted in the emergence of churches for homosexual Christians. Those who speak, dress or behave differently from the majority can be made to feel uncomfortable. Many working-class Christians are uneasy in predominantly middle-class church culture; homeless people present unsettling challenges to suburban congregations; and post-modernists struggle with churches designed and run by modernists.

A teenager walked into the church service. He had no previous experience of church and knew nobody there. They were pleased to see him and eager to make him feel welcome, but he was profoundly deaf.

They rose to the challenge admirably. Two church members learned sign language and could soon communicate well with him. And the whole church learned part of the communion liturgy in sign language so they could include this young man fully in their central act of worship.

A wonderful example of an inherited church stretching culturally to embrace someone different, but what if the next person is blind, and the next speaks no English, and the next is a gypsy, and the next works nights and is never free on Sunday mornings, and the next . . .

How far can any church stretch in a plural culture?

A convicted sex offender began to attend the village church, looking for a community within which to grow in his faith. His past was known only to the minister. He was welcomed into the church community, which was a safe space because no children attended the church. But what if a family with young children started coming?

Another church responded to the plea of a converted paedophile for help resisting temptation by setting up an intensive pastoral support network that meant he had 24/7 support. He was never left alone. But for how many paedophiles could they provide this level of support?

Or should a church for paedophiles be set up?

Churches for deaf people, homeless people, recovering drug abusers or alcoholics, ex-offenders, New Age travellers, people with mental health problems: the alternative if the church is not to neglect those often marginalised by society is for inherited church to include everyone. But what a challenge! In many cases there is no desire to exclude people, but the cost of inclusion is high if this involves the church making changes rather than new-comers learning to fit in. In a plural and fragmented society, inclusive churches may be stretched in many directions by diversity in their local community. Churches reaching out to and specialising in responding to marginalised communities may also be needed.

Indigenous neighbourhood churches

But incarnating church into different cultures is not an issue only for network-oriented churches, nor should we infer that network churches have supplanted neighbourhood churches.[96] Geographical communities are still widespread: fifty per cent of adults live within thirty minutes of their mothers; fifty-two per cent see their mothers weekly; forty-two per cent see their fathers weekly. In many areas local community remains fundamentally important, or if it is fragmenting churches might perceive their mission as working to restore community life. Furthermore, over-emphasis on network churches would further disadvantage poor communities whose access to networks beyond the local area is limited. Whole urban or rural communities might be marginalised.

Too many church planters in the 1990s assumed they knew what kind of church to plant before they started. Imposing pre-determined models of church on communities rather than acting as catalysts in the emergence of truly indigenous neighbourhood churches produced exotic plants that failed to sink deep roots into the community. This is a perennial problem, one reason for the historic weakness of churches in inner-city communities, which are unimpressed by efforts to impose suburban churches run by middle-class or upper-class leaders.

We should not assume emerging churches are immune to this temptation. Those who are convinced that cell church, seeker-oriented church or any other model is always appropriate will be liable to impose their chosen expression. Those searching for a post-modern form of church or exploring alternative worship may be more concerned about their own cultural preferences than the needs of others beyond the church.

Reshaping church for mission means we start with the mission context not the church: missiology precedes ecclesiology. The term 'emerging church' should indicate this. Authentic churches emerge from interaction between the gospel and different cultural contexts. They are not designed by exchanging ideas on websites or in conferences on emerging church; they take shape in the costly incarnational ministry of cross-cultural missionaries who immerse themselves in communities.

This is the attitude and approach of many who are involved in incarnating church into various networks and sub-cultures. It is also a core value of those involved in a new wave of emerging urban churches. Two networks embodying this indigenous strategy are *Urban Neighbours of Hope* in Australia[97] and *Urban Expression* (an urban mission agency with Anabaptist values) in Britain.[98]

The team wondered what the church they were planting would be called. They had decided to wait until local people named it. Naming implied ownership and they wanted the church to be indigenous rather than imposed.

In fact, they had not even used the term 'church' to describe what was emerging and they called themselves 'followers of Jesus' rather than Christians in a community with many Muslims to whom 'Christian' generally meant 'Western'.

Eventually local people said the church needed a name – and were surprised to hear this was up to them. The name they chose was simple, geographical and resonated with the community's history. It was not a name the planting team had considered!

Andrew Hamilton reflects on a shift in the thinking of emerging churches. Tracing various stages on the journey he concludes: 'There has been some "success" in each of these stages, but I have a sense that they are each fundamentally flawed in that they seem to suggest that if we get the worship gathering happening right then the people will come. It suggests that missiology follows ecclesiology.'[99]

Identifying the latest stage as 'Incarnational Faith Communities' or 'Emerging Missional Church', he continues: 'I sense this is where many of us are at today. The key difference between this arrangement and its predecessors is that IFCs seek to understand the culture first, *then* do mission and *from there* create worshiping communities. It is a go to them approach rather than a come to us – a fundamental reconfiguration of the DNA. It recognises that getting the meeting right is not the answer to the missional woes of the church, but that what we need to do is incarnate the gospel in our communities and then grow churches – in whatever form they may take – from there.'

This perspective differentiates some models in this chapter from many in the previous chapter. Whether the focus is networks or neighbourhoods, the strategy has shifted from 'church *for* the unchurched' (which often means de-churched or semi-churched) to 'church *from* the unchurched', building on a different foundation and allowing pre-churched people to shape what emerges. If the former model requires larger churches and huge resources, the latter works best with tiny teams and minimal resources.

An Anabaptist postscript

How might Anabaptists reflect on the models presented here?

- Churches need no special buildings and can gather wherever Christians are.

- Those on the margins should receive priority attention from the people of God.
- Reconciliation and inclusivity are essential gospel reflexes for disciples.
- Effective inter-generational processes are crucial for the pilgrim church.
- Cultural attunement needs to be balanced by counter-cultural witness.
- Bottom-up grass-roots strategies are consistent with the biblical story.
- Subversive missionary approaches are preferable to imperialistic invitational models.

6

Reconfiguring Community

What do we mean by mission?

A question many readers may be asking is what mission means in emerging churches. Some may suspect from the last two chapters that in many, or even most, mission is narrowly defined in terms of evangelism and church growth.

Given the evangelical background and convictions of many participants in emerging churches this would be unsurprising. Twentieth century evangelicals (unlike their forebears) tended to equate mission with evangelism or, at least, to assert its priority among the church's tasks. And some models imported from other cultures are rooted in similar theological assumptions and dependent on evangelical church growth ideology. This tendency persists in some, but by no means all, emerging churches.

However, during the final quarter of the twentieth century many evangelicals in inherited churches recovered a more holistic model of mission that inspired earlier evangelicals, and this perspective has been embraced by many (though not all) emerging churches. For some, a holistic approach was a factor prompting their emergence from a narrow evangelicalism; for others this has developed as churches have emerged in contexts where inherited ways of thinking can be challenged. Indeed, perhaps by way of reaction, in some emerging churches there is a tendency to exclude evangelism from any definition of mission.

Holistic mission typifies churches in the final category in the last chapter – indigenous neighbourhood churches. These are less prescriptive about their understanding of church and allow their perception of what God is doing in their neighbourhood to shape the church as they try to discern what mission means in their community. This category might legitimately have appeared in this chapter. But holistic mission is also discernible in other expressions of church in Chapter 5 and even in churches that have adopted models examined in Chapter 4.

What do we mean by community?

The thread running through the stories in this chapter is 'community', but (as with 'mission') different groups use this term differently. Some emerging churches have been profoundly impacted by engaging with their neighbours or with the community encountered through their relational networks. They have reconfigured their own community life as they have listened to the wider community, discerned its rhythms, made friends, found ways to participate in it and developed partnerships to respond to needs within the community. Through their engagement they have recognised the cultural chasm between church and community and have searched for new ways of being church in their context.

Churches from different traditions have been challenged and reconfigured in this way, stirred to think anew about how to incarnate the gospel where they are, with profound implications for their structure, ethos and activities. Whatever their missiology, a 'go' mentality and a flexible and open approach to the inter-relationship of church and community are reshaping these churches.

Other emerging churches have been stimulated by reflection on – and sometimes deep dissatisfaction with – the community life experienced in inherited church. This is a frequent complaint of church leavers, unsatisfied by institutional forms of belonging and insipid expressions of 'fellowship', and longing for deeper friendships and more authentic community. This concern has also motivated others, who have not left church but have yearned for forms of community that will sustain them spiritually and relationally in ways they have not experienced through a programmatic proliferation of impersonal meetings.

As in previous chapters, the following models are as different from one other as any of them are from inherited church. There are shared values and practices – not least the significance of *size* and *food* – but many different expressions of community life. Nor does the appearance of a particular model here imply it is non-missional: as we continue to emphasise, we are offering a tentative and inadequate categorisation of emerging church.

Churches shaped by community engagement

Although many churches in Britain are growing numerically (about a quarter grew in the 1990s) and some denominations are registering growth, statistics indicate relentless decline in the numbers participating in Sunday services. Projections suggest participation could be as low as 4.4 per cent by 2020 and 2 per cent by 2040.[100]

However, the English Church Attendance Survey in 1998 revealed that, while regular attendance on Sundays amounted to 7.5 per cent of the population, another 7.5 per cent participated in other church activities. Some attended Sunday services less often; others enjoyed *Songs of Praise*; others again had accepted invitations to *Alpha*[101] or similar courses. And 2.4 per cent participated in midweek church activities but not Sunday services.[102]

These midweek activities vary enormously: groups for parents and toddlers, senior citizens' activities, youth events, children's clubs, special interest groups, music and dance groups, cafés and arts projects, counselling services and many others. Some are run by churches; others are independent but use church buildings and involve church members and others. In some communities church buildings provide valuable public meeting spaces, which host many different organisations. Elsewhere, multi-purpose buildings enable churches to offer suitable facilities to the wider community.

Although activities range from the creative and costly to the mundane and moribund, many churches' track records are impressive and local communities value them. We can cynically dismiss the stated commitment of various political parties to develop partnerships with churches and other faith-based groups as attempts to win votes or achieve the delivery of services more cheaply than through other agencies. There are certainly dangers of churches naively imagining they are exercising social and political influence when actually they are being co-opted. But politicians would not woo churches at all if they did not recognise the extent and effectiveness of their involvement in local communities.

Problems are not uncommon, especially around issues of control and whether some activities are permissible on church premises. But these midweek activities represent the desire of many churches to engage with their community and are significant points of contact between churches and those not involved on Sundays. For most churches, too, such activities are perceived as mission, although the motivation and expectations are not always clear or agreed. For some, midweek activities are ways churches can serve their community, enhance personal and family well-being, develop creativity, address local issues and foster stronger community spirit. For others, such activities are not only worthwhile in themselves but opportunities for faith-sharing and stepping stones into the church. They hope some will move from midweek events into Sunday services.

Several questions should be asked about churches' community involvement:

- Can churches hold together initiatives that serve their community without strings attached *and* efforts to share their faith with participants in church-based or church-related activities? Must any attempt to do so be manipulative, or is a truly holistic model of mission possible?

- In a situation of persistent decline, how long can churches sustain community activities unless they recruit new members/workers? Reluctance to evangelise is understandable given very crass examples in some churches, but this may be institutionally suicidal and precipitate the collapse of the churches' community engagement.

- Should we abandon any expectation that participants in midweek activities will also participate in Sunday services? Some will make this transition, but for many their only connection with church will be participating in what many church members designate ancillary events.

- How do we interpret situations where churches start community projects but allow or encourage them to develop with diminishing connections to the sponsoring congregation? Are these healthy models of giving resources away to the community and building local partnerships, or missed opportunities for churches to be transformed and renewed by community engagement?

Community engagement represents a potential growing edge for churches, both in their self-understanding and their ability to reproduce and thereby sustain community engagement in the future. Some emerging churches can be interpreted as experimental responses to these questions.

Midweek church

Some churches realise that many people who participate in midweek activities will not attend Sunday services. In the hope that some will respond positively to sensitive encouragement to explore issues of faith, they are developing midweek church.

Midweek church differs from midweek services, which have been traditional in many churches but are hard to sustain with declining numbers and changed patterns of work and family. Midweek church is an expression of 'go' rather than 'come' thinking, an attempt to create church around activities and groups happening during the week. It recognises that, for many, attendance on Sundays is inconvenient or even impossible due to other commitments – even if they were willing to venture into an unknown and culturally alien environment; but it believes some will share the contemporary renewal of interest in spirituality and might welcome the incorporation of new elements into their midweek activities. Rather than persisting with the vain hope that some will eventually make the transition to Sunday services, midweek church builds church around and for people already involved in church-based activities.

Midweek churches are emerging from various midweek activities and from inherited churches of diverse traditions. *Mission-shaped Church* recognises this may commend itself particularly to Anglo-Catholic churches, many of which already have midweek services. The step from these to midweek church serving those who do not participate on Sundays is significant but feasible.

The report retells the story first published in 2002 in *Transmission* (the Bible Society magazine) of a priest who inherited a poorly-attended Wednesday morning Eucharist that began to grow through the participation of others with no connection to Sunday services. As he renounced his attempt to focus everything on Sundays and invested in this midweek form of church, numbers trebled and included many who never attended Sunday services, and a monthly house group developed to nurture participants in the midweek congregation.[103]

A church with a multi-faceted creative arts project on its premises involving hundreds of people each week in multiple activities, the vast majority of whom have no link with the Sunday congregation, has established a Wednesday lunchtime Eucharist incorporated into a shared meal. This has become 'church' for some who work in the project and others who participate in its activities. There is a regular core group, who are joined by different people each week in an open and inclusive gathering.[104]

We should perhaps include here (although they are not really the result of community engagement) midweek churches that have not emerged from midweek activities or to create church among people not involved in Sunday services, but as alternatives for existing church members. We could regard such alternative services as nothing more than extra midweek meetings, common in many churches over many years, but the experience of some churches is that these may develop into full-orbed congregations and offer opportunities for spiritual growth and experimentation that has potential for renewing the Sunday congregation too.

The Church in Wales' website tells the story of *Y Wednesday* at St Anne's Church, Rhyl. This is a midweek congregation that has failed to attract people from beyond the church, despite initial hopes, but has been a source of renewal and empowerment for the 70 people who participate in a service that allows room for experimentation and greater participation than they experience on Sundays. The vicar describes this midweek church as 'an alternative way of people being able to express their faith, a way that isn't restricted by Anglican traditional structures.'[105]

Project church

Churches involved in various community projects, as initiators or partners with other agencies, have sometimes been deeply affected by this experience. 'It may be through community ministry that a radical reassessment of church life begins.'[106] Community engagement challenges their theological ideas, priorities, expectations, values and commitments. They may also find their perceptions of church significantly impacted, as they ponder the cultural gap between the church and the community with whom they have been interacting, or as they discover relationships between people outside the church that seem deeper and richer than relationships within it.

For some Christians, community engagement becomes an alternative to participation in inherited church. It feels more earthed, holistic, authentic and relevant. For them the project becomes 'church'. Some peace workers and justice activists effectively view their gatherings as church.

For others, the ecclesial implications of their involvement in community projects need to be shared and wrestled with. In November 2002 The Shaftesbury Society organised a consultation, *Concrete Faith*, for representatives of churches involved in over forty local community projects. Although it included the sharing of best practice, updates on government regulations and informal networking, its first stated aim was 'to create a forum to discuss key questions that are arising about what is church in the twentyfirst century.' The executive report notes the 'prophetic challenge' of the projects and their organisers' conviction they are 'part of a wider move of God to challenge and change the shape of the church.'[107]

He was passionate about issues of justice and had focused on the needs of homeless people in a city in the Midlands. An irritant to the systems and structures he felt were bureaucratic and cumbersome, he 'got things done' and developed a project that cared for, accommodated and served hundreds of homeless people. He was a Christian but impatient with the churches for their half-hearted involvement in the community; the project was really his church. Once a week it hosted a contemplative worship service for homeless people, but really he saw the whole project as what 'church' should be.

Chris Erskine, exploring the implications of what was shared, challenges the inherited structures of 'concentric church', which hinder Christians uniting around missional activities and working together effectively.[108] He advocates 'locality church', within which ecclesial structures are much lighter and more liberating. Some are exploring this approach. A report at the 2002 Building Bridges of Hope conference resonated with this way of thinking, describing attempts in the Bradford inner ring area to pool resources and transcend concentric structures, though this has not been as effective as some anticipated. No doubt other experiments and models will emerge as Christians ponder ways community projects might renew inherited churches.

Churches may also emerge from projects, accidentally or by design.

The story of *Living Proof* was told in two publications in 1999 and 2000. One account summarised what had happened thus:

'Living Proof was originally just a good example of Christian community work (an approach to youth work which involves teaching life skills to young people through teaching them to care for younger young people), but the children began to see staff meeting for prayer and asked to join them.

'Young people became Christians on Living Proof weeks, but where could they go for discipleship? They did not fit into local churches. Soon there were too many to fit in a house and they started meeting in a community centre. It was never their intention, but they discovered they had a church.'[109]

The story of the *Hope Community* in Wolverhampton has also been told in various places:

'Three Roman Catholic religious sisters were asked by their parish church to conduct a community survey in Heath Town, Wolverhampton – a nine tower-block estate with much social need. The sisters went into the estate every day and simply listened to people's pain and despair.

'As time went by, they felt increasingly ill at ease returning to their own house in a comfortable suburb and eventually rented a maisonette on the third floor of one of the tower blocks . . . Their presence catalysed many social changes, although they did not set out to initiate anything.

'Estate services have begun – planned and led by local people. Computer courses have started, holidays, celebrations, literacy training have all improved the quality of life. Their strength of community has been central to this way of being church. Their small community has helped create greater community in the wider and otherwise dysfunctional setting. The sisters would not publicly call what happens "church", but members of the local community perceive the third floor maisonette as the chapel for the estate.'[110]

How is 'project church' different from 'enterprise church' in the last chapter? There is considerable overlap, but it seemed worth differentiating them to explore the different dynamics community projects have set in motion for various Christians and churches. Perhaps enterprise church appeals more strongly to evangelical churches and project churches are more congenial to Christians from other traditions, but this distinction should not be pushed too far. After a while, the various models blend into each other, especially given the particular characteristics of any stories we tell.

Seven-day-a-week church

'Project church' also blends into this next category. Some churches have initiated projects that become so extensive and all-embracing it is difficult to know where church stops and project begins, or vice versa. Unlike examples mentioned earlier, where a church starts a project but remains largely separate and unaffected by it, or even where churches are significantly reshaped by their projects, some churches have developed a seven-day-a-week understanding of church. Even to ask where church stops and the project begins may be to miss the radical reshaping and re-imagining of church that is happening.

This question may assume church consists essentially in worship services and other traditional ecclesial activities, alongside which community projects run. But the seven-day-a-week model challenges this assumption and suggests church is fluid and multi-faceted. Two examples appear in another book in this series. Jeanne Hinton recounts her visit to Orbiston neighbourhood centre, Glasgow, and her conversation with the minister of Zion Baptist Church, Cambridge (a church involved in Building Bridges of Hope). Comments from those involved reveal how their understanding of church has shifted.

Eileen Gibson, Projects Director at Orbiston, acknowledging that not all members of the congregation were fully involved in the neighbourhood centre and that some were disappointed that Sunday attendances had not grown, indicated her commitment to a different model: 'You can see it as church happening here for a few one hour on Sunday, or as happening here seven days a week for many.'[111] To the question 'How many members does Zion Baptist Church have?' the answer was: 'Well, there are over 250 project volunteers.'[112]

But the tendency for links between the worshipping community and such initiatives gradually to be eroded raises questions about the sustainability of such open-edged forms of church. And converting church buildings into community centres may not be interpreted by the local community as churches hope. Ann Morisy also warns: 'rather than being perceived as a new way of being church . . . opening up our churches for community use can feed into the dominant view that churches are failing.'[113]

These models of church shaped by community engagement all in different ways add fuel to the fire as we continue to ask 'what is church?' Many present an expression of church more open at the edges than many inherited churches. They chime in well with contemporary discussions about 'believing' and 'belonging'. They pose challenging questions about the extent to which inherited churches are struggling to relate to their community because they start with church rather than the community as they attempt to incarnate the gospel.[114]

Post-Alpha church

Another expression of emerging church is the phenomenon of churches developing from *Alpha* courses. These could be located in an earlier chapter dealing with churches resulting from mission initiatives, especially since their missiology tends to prioritise evangelism. But they share some characteristics with churches shaped by their community engagement. In particular, the *Alpha* experience has (like the experience of community projects) raised questions about the model of church with which organisers are familiar.

We cannot examine in detail here the theology of *Alpha*, criticisms levelled against it, reasons for its extraordinary success in diverse contexts or questions about its capacity to engage with a society moving further away from Christendom. But three factors in the course's popularity and effectiveness have been:

- The emphasis on friendship and sharing faith relationally.
- The relaxed environment created by the meal that begins each session.
- The opportunity for dialogue, questions and the freedom to disagree.

A difficulty many have encountered is that these factors are less apparent in churches which those who respond positively to *Alpha* are expected to join! The relaxed and friendly environment has morphed into an institution with multiple meetings where relationships seem superficial. Unlike *Alpha*, where teaching precedes opportunities to ask questions, explore issues and express dissent, monologue sermons with no right of reply are ubiquitous. Tea and biscuits are poor substitutes for the meals that made the course so enjoyable.

There have been different responses to this mismatch. Some have been unwilling to make changes and have been disappointed by the drop-out rate between the end of *Alpha* and involvement in 'proper church'. Others have allowed the way they operate to be reshaped by the practices and ethos of *Alpha* (as other churches have allowed their community engagement to reshape them). And in some places, especially where inherited churches are unwilling or unable to adapt, new churches are emerging from *Alpha* courses.[115]

Churches shaped by community dynamics

But it is not just those who come to faith through *Alpha* who struggle with the community dynamics of inherited church. Church leavers speak frequently of their dismay at the lack of authentic community and their yearning for something deeper and more rounded. The experience of *food, friendship* and *freedom to question* which *Alpha* participants enjoy but often miss in churches is also significant for church leavers. Listening to those on the way into church and on the way out reveals many echoes and much common ground!

In this section we continue to explore the influence of 'community' in the emerging church, but our focus shifts from engagement with the wider community to questions and concerns about the kind of community experienced in the churches themselves. This need not imply these models lack missional impetus: indeed, some are strongly mission-oriented. But their choice of a particular way of being church is influenced by concerns that inherited church offers expressions of community that are neither attractive to those with whom they are sharing faith nor sustaining existing members.

Some stories, however, are of 'recovery churches', designed to reconnect with church leavers and re-establish a communal dimension among those who would otherwise be isolated followers of Jesus. By no means all leavers are interested in such churches, suspicious they may quickly revert to the institutional mode with which they have become disenchanted, or even unsure if any kind of communal Christianity is worth pursuing. If some models in the last section probe the link between 'belonging' and 'believing', some of these models question whether over the long haul 'believing' is possible without 'belonging'.

Churches emerging from discontent with the quality of community life in inherited churches can, of course, be inward-looking rather than missional (especially given the aversion to certain forms of mission in some groups). But some would argue renewing the community life of churches is a crucial pre-requisite for effective and sustainable mission. We can bear this in mind as we investigate more emerging churches.

Table church

Many inherited churches have endured long and often bitter disputes about seating arrangements. Whether to replace the pews with chairs, what kinds of chairs, which way they should face and how they should be arranged has occupied an inordinate amount of internal church discussion. The spirit in which this discussion sometimes takes place and the self-interest that often inspires opinions have contributed to the disillusionment of church members who feel they can no longer identify with a community that behaves in this way.

An apparently facetious response to this debate is that churches are asking the wrong question. First, decide where the table belongs and then place the chairs around it! Behind this comment is a more serious suggestion that church happens best around a table and in the context of a meal – that the *Alpha* model is appropriate not just for introductory courses but for church. In various places, table churches are emerging, restoring church to the domestic setting within which it began and, some argue, still belongs.

A young inner-city church meets each Sunday evening around a table, sharing a meal, breaking bread and drinking wine together in remembrance of Jesus and praying for each other and their local community.

Their conversation might range over individual activities in which they are involved during the week as teacher, social worker, church planter, project worker, mother or bus driver. Or they might explore ways of serving the community in which they are working for the emergence of an indigenous neighbourhood church.

What about teaching? The church runs short courses on a midweek evening. What will happen as the church outgrows the table? It can set up another table church.

She had not belonged to any church for several years, having left her church at a time of great pain and struggle. But she had welcomed the invitation to participate in a table church and had taken part actively in all that happened. She seemed to feel at home, but we were uncertain until she told us over the washing up (a vital aspect of table church) that she was usually 'allergic' to Christians but had really enjoyed the evening.

Table church is not simply church meeting in a home after a shared meal, as many home groups and some other emerging churches do. Wary of the changed atmosphere, demise of laughter and conversation, more formal approach and stilted religiosity that can result from moving from dining room to lounge, table churches remain around the table. Some perceive this setting as a contextual reaction to a culture in which TV dinners and individualised 'grazing' has so superseded dining together that many homes now lack a dining table.

Others argue this form of church is modelled on the life of Jesus, who spent so much time at various tables his opponents accused him of being a glutton and a drunkard.[116] They note the symbolism of shared meals in several parables and the significance of eating together throughout the Gospels, not least John framing Jesus' public ministry with a wedding feast and an evening meal, with a post-resurrection beach barbecue thrown in for good measure.[117] They point to the early Christians' agapé meals and the celebration of the Eucharist in the context of a meal.

The prospect of church services lasting for three hours is normal in some cultures, but most inherited churches would find this uncongenial. That a dinner party might last for three hours, however, is well within normal cultural expectations. Table churches blend many components: words of welcome, good food, *lectio divina*, candles and night lights, fine wine, prayers for the church and the world, animated conversation, set prayers and songs, Bible reading and theological discussion, sharing of bread and wine, washing up together and words of dismissal. Several use 'table liturgies' that interweave these elements, valuing the combination of formal structure and informal setting.

Household church

Table church is limited not only by the size of the table but by group dynamics. More than twelve participants mean multiple conversations develop and it is hard to sustain the cohesion of church together around the table. But table church is one expression of a recovery of small-scale church emerging across western culture. Others are cell church, home church, base ecclesial community and small Christian community.[118] The origins of the New Churches were in homes but as these grew most expanded out of homes and reverted to more traditional forms of church. Not all are convinced this trajectory is helpful.

A term some use who are committed to retaining small-scale church despite growing numbers is *household church*. The strategy is to limit the community to the size of a household (which will vary in different contexts) and to multiply households rather than expanding out of homes. Many of these churches also encourage their members to participate in larger gatherings (as with cell churches), either ecumenically or through joint meetings of several households. But the focus of church life is in the households. The key difference from cell churches is that household churches are less rigidly structured and more flexible.

The Crowded House in Sheffield is a missional network of household churches. An article on its website uses the metaphor of homelessness to interpret contemporary western culture and asks: 'how can we be church so that we are that home to the homeless that God wants us to be?'

It continues: 'The Crowded House is an attempt at providing an answer to that question. Many of the people who are most vociferous in their rejection of traditional expressions of Christianity are often the ones who feel most keenly the sense of homelessness already described. By doing church this way, which means taking the idea of family as the defining metaphor, meeting in homes, and being built around the household model, we are able to be that home that people need without the necessary structures of larger, more institutional expressions of church.

'It also gives us great freedom in terms of making the gospel our defining activity, and places us in a great position to meet the needs of those who know something of this homelessness, and ensures that they are in a better position to listen to the diagnosis of their condition, and respond to the remedy.

'Obviously, this need for home isn't something that disappears once we become Christians, and household church is a great environment to learn what it means to be the people of God, and to enjoy being "home from home" as together we actively wait for that "home of righteousness" which is our inheritance.'[119]

Small-scale churches offer intimate forms of community and are clearly attractive to many people, but they provoke significant questions, to some of which participants have carefully considered answers:

- Are they too small and fragile to be sustainable or missionally effective?

- Even if they are not homogeneous, do they contain sufficient diversity to foster growth in discipleship?

- Are they so intimate as to be threatening to those who want to explore the Christian faith in a less intense environment?

- Can one encounter the transcendence as well as the immanence of God around the dining table?

- What kinds of community engagement can such churches undertake and how can they participate in ecumenical relationships?

- What forms of leadership, accountability and interdependence are fostered in and through such churches?

But there is evidence that, contrary to popular perceptions, small inherited churches have greater growth potential than large churches.[120] In a post-modern culture which prefers small-scale, grass-roots activities to larger organisations, small-scale church – inherited or emerging – may be appropriate. For marginal post-Christendom churches, this may be authentic and essential.

Organic church

Even though small-scale expressions of church are informal, relaxed and capable of considerable spontaneity, for some Christians they are still perceived as organised rather than organic. Some have embarked on a journey towards a still simpler form of church, gradually dismantling institutional aspects of church in the hope of finding authentic and participative community. Some call this *organic church*, others *simple church* ('micro-church' and 'pocket church' are also occasionally used).

There are, inevitably, dangers inherent in this approach: where does one stop, and can any community survive without some supporting structures? I have dialogued with two groups on this journey and was beginning to label them *deconstructed church* in my classification of emerging church. Both, however, have deconstructed themselves out of existence!

But the desire for organic expressions of church, especially in post-modern culture that is averse to institutions and wary of pretensions of permanence, remains strong. A website run by 'a group of church planters/leaders seeking to discover what church might mean within the context of our emerging generation(s)' defines organic church as 'an attempt to get behind the additives and preservatives that we've attached to the institution we call "Church" and discover how the living body of Christ might flourish if allowed to grow naturally.'[121] And, in different ways, the concept of *liquid church* and 'Natural Church Development' both use organic concepts and terminology.[122]

Solace is one of six congregations of St Hilary's Anglican Church in Melbourne. It consists of about 200 people of all ages. Unlike the others, this is an experimental congregation, exploring the implications of being 'organic church'.

Committed to 'normative principles and practices rather than normative structures and abstract beliefs', and confident 'healthy relationships are self-organising', this church functions as a catalyst, offering 'a context for groups to emerge'.

Two images used to describe how this church operates are: a flock of geese in flight with rotating leadership; and 'downloading a virus' to build community and impart core values organically.

Post-church communities

Another expression of organic church is the emergence of groups for church leavers, who are uninterested in returning to 'church' but want to meet with Christians on spiritual journeys similar to their own.

The models we have considered in this chapter connect effectively with different groups of people. Midweek church tends to serve the semi-churched; project church has the capacity to engage with the pre-churched or anti-churched; post-*Alpha* church is for the pre-churched. Table church may attract the pre-churched or post-churched; some household churches are missional and reach out to pre-churched or de-churched people.

With the exception of some table churches, these models do not connect well with post-churched people, although in structure and ethos some small-scale and organic churches may be more congenial. But post-church groups are emerging, some through the influence of catalysts, others spontaneously as post-church people discover one another and begin to share their lives and questions.[123]

Some are groups of post-evangelicals[124] meeting to ask questions they could not ask in evangelical churches, explore issues of faith and culture, debunk the evangelical sub-culture from which they are alienated and reflect on life after church. These may be simply discussion groups, offering much-needed freedom and friendship, although some beg the question of whether it is possible to be post-evangelical without being grumpy! Other groups move beyond this reactive stage and develop into post-church communities that offer ongoing support and resources for post-churched people.

According to its website, '*holy joes* was begun around 1989 by a group of Christians who wanted to meet but were disenchanted with church. They outgrew the basement room they initially met in and decided that a local pub was the most logical place to meet; after all pubs were the centre of a community and besides which they sold beer. Holy Joes meets on Tuesdays at 8pm upstairs in the Bag O'Nails pub on Buckingham Palace Road in Victoria. The group exists to provide discussion and spirituality in a mainly (but not entirely) Christian context. We seek to encourage honest and open debate in an atmosphere where everyone's views are respected. We also respect any individual's decision to opt out of a discussion or part of a discussion.'[125]

A helpful guide in this area is Alan Jamieson, whose careful research, interviews with church leavers, interpretation of the issues involved and reflections on the spiritual journeys of leavers have helped many church leaders and leavers understand what is happening.[126] He reports: 'most . . . of the people interviewed went on to form or find post-church groups in which they could belong and share their faith,' and comments: 'institutional Churches and post-church groups may meet for similar purposes: to worship, to pray, to teach and be taught and to share the sacraments. What makes the post-church groups different isn't a theological or functional difference; rather, the differences are linked to culture and values . . . Such groups not only *allow*, but actively *encourage* people to question, explore and search beyond the boundaries of discussions and teaching set down implicitly or explicitly in institutional forms of EPC church.'[127] Though recognising their limitations and struggles, Jamieson suggests post-church groups may not only be connecting places for church leavers but pointers towards the future shape of the church in western culture.

An Anabaptist postscript

The Anabaptist tradition has been a stimulus or resource to some emerging churches attempting to reconfigure community. Indeed, the Anabaptist emphasis on community has been a primary factor attracting Christians from diverse traditions. Anabaptist influences are particularly evident in several table churches and in discussions about organic church; and recently post-churched people have gravitated to Anabaptist events. They have been drawn to the unusually ecumenical but radical Anabaptist approach as an alternative to vague liberalism, narrow evangelicalism or post-evangelical despondency.

Anabaptist perspectives interact with the above models in various ways that provide a useful conclusion to this chapter, highlighting issues for inherited as well as emerging churches:

- Early Anabaptists rejected the need for special days or special buildings. They initiated simpler expressions of church, often in domestic settings, that needed less institutional paraphernalia.

- Some Anabaptists have questioned whether certain community practices the New Testament commends (sharing resources, church discipline, multi-voiced worship) are feasible in large churches.

- A central Anabaptist motif is 'following' or 'journeying', and 'emerging church tends to think rather more concretely of "following Jesus" than of being converted.'[128]

- Anabaptism combines clear core convictions and openness to fresh revelation. This undergirds the 'centred-set' approach many emerging churches value.[129]

- Although deeply concerned to develop authentic community life, Anabaptism is fundamentally mission-oriented and challenges churches that lack this dimension.

- Anabaptists would urge those involved in these emerging churches to consider the implications of post-Christendom as well as post-modernity.

7

Re-imagining Worship

Worship wars

Many inherited churches have experienced 'worship wars'; some have suffered pain, division and disorientation as a result. Many New Churches, especially in the 1970s and 1980s, emerged from such conflicts. As arguments raged about the nature, style and culture of worship, feelings ran high

Some Christians were unwilling to sacrifice familiar and much-loved liturgical forms. They contrasted the depth, range and beauty of music, prayers, words and symbols that had sustained churches over many generations with modern alternatives that seemed crass, repetitive and aesthetically impoverished. Reluctant to admit inherited forms might also have limitations and were not sustaining the present generation, many mounted determined, and not always gracious, resistance to change.

Other Christians found these new expressions of worship liberating and exhilarating. They revelled in greater informality, fresh rhythms and different instruments, triumphant praise and intimate phraseology, the manifestation of spiritual gifts and emergence of bands and worship leaders. Confident this was restoration of New Testament worship, they were not surprised when churches adopting this worship style grew. Many rejoiced that their children, raised in this context, would not need to fight the same battles.

These Christians have been shocked to discover their teenage children are often as bored and uninspired by their preferred style of worship as they were by an older style. Some are abandoning churches where 'new' expressions of worship have stagnated, multiple participation has reverted to front-led performance, spiritual gifts have atrophied and extended monotone and monochrome singing sessions are all that remain. Others have returned to inherited churches, newly appreciative of liturgical resources and rhythms against which their parents reacted so strongly. Some are less enthusiastic but, unable with integrity to stay where they are, have transferred to inherited churches rather than abandon-ing church altogether.

This turmoil over worship styles, which we must interpret in light of changes and fragmentation in contemporary culture, has prompted the development of another group of emerging churches. Content with neither inherited forms of worship nor the style that has pervaded many churches since the 1970s, they are exploring alternative possibilities. In this chapter we will consider emerging churches that are re-imagining worship.

Again we acknowledge limitations in our classification. Re-imagining worship has been a feature of some emerging churches in earlier chapters. Household churches and cell churches recover and encourage the multi-voiced ethos introduced but not sus-tained by the 1970s worship renewal. Seeker-oriented churches choreograph events that require minimal participation and are culturally attuned to the anticipated audience (audience rather than congregation). Table churches blend informality and multiple participation with various liturgical forms.

Significant mission and community dynamics are also apparent in many models here, questioning their allocation to this chapter. But re-imagining worship, liturgy and spirituality has played a shaping role in what is emerging.

Alternative worship

Although emerging church cannot be regarded as a movement, 'alternative worship' (or 'alt.worship') displays characteristics of a movement or a developing network.[130] Some groups have been around longer than other emerging churches; many have websites linked to one another. There is extensive informal networking and sharing of ideas; the annual Greenbelt Festival is a high-profile connecting point. Several books interpret this phenome-non and offer liturgical resources.[131] Consequently, and perhaps also because alt.worship elements are found in other emerging churches, 'emerging church' is sometimes (though unhelpfully) regarded as coterminous with 'alternative worship'.

Steve Taylor defines alt.worship as 'liturgical innovation char-acterised by communal participation, employment of popular cultural resources, a rediscovery of ancient liturgy and an appreci-ation of creativity and the arts.'[132] Characteristic features include:

- An emphasis on space, environment, ambience and context.

- A creative use of diverse technologies, multi-media, the arts and symbolism.

- A multi-directional, individualised and decentred approach.

- An eclectic use of liturgical resources from many times and places.

- A participative ethos, wary about leadership, concerned about process.

- A recovery of ritual to encourage multi-sensory, embodied encounters.[133]

- An open-ended experience, allowing multiple interpretations.

- A preference for story-telling over monologue sermons.

- A reflective and contemplative mood, evoking wonder, even awe.

- Openness to experimentation and an attitude of provisionality.

Alt.worship has been interpreted as an attempt to recombine three essential elements of worship: mystery, hospitality and participation.[134] Stimuli for its emergence include: disillusionment with evangelical/charismatic spirituality and the associated sub-culture (most participants are from this background); a desire to integrate faith and contemporary culture in an authentic and contextualised worshipping community; a missional thrust into a generation of young adults alienated from the churches; and engagement with post-modernity and theological issues this has placed on the agenda. According to Jonny Baker, alt.worship attempts to remove the dislocation of worship from the rest of life by 'bringing the real world into church and taking church back into the real world.'[135]

A founding member describes the origins and motivation of an alt.worship group in London:

'*Vaux* started in 1998, basically in response to being bored in church! Sitting in pews, singing 'light-rock'

> songs, listening to long orations . . . didn't fit with who we felt we were as people . . . rather than give up on the whole thing, which we saw so many doing, we decided to try to do something about it.
>
> '*Vaux* is essentially about worship. We have come to see that to worship with integrity you have to give some-thing of yourself – something that has integrity for you as a person or community. So the only reason we have great video and graphics stuff is because there are people who are into that . . . similarly with the dance, theatre, liturgy, installations, readings, music and food that have sometimes formed part of services . . . We are not looking for every church in the country getting into banging house music and mad visuals . . . rather that people see that worship is an offering that has to come from the heart, and that that will mean different things for different communities.'[136]

The remarkably creative but eventually disastrous Nine O'Clock Service in Sheffield in the 1990s was seminal. Some drew on experience in youth work and experiments with 'rave services'. Others reacted against performance-oriented worship and the 'worship leader' cult, adopting instead the perspective Eddie Gibbs describes as true worship: 'God is the audience, not the congregation, and those who lead worship are not the centre-stage performers but the off-stage prompters and facilitators.'[137] Many castigated the limited range and often banal content of many songs and extemporary prayers. In much evangelical/charismatic worship they detected overemphasis on immanence at the expense of transcendence and a general loss of mystery. They also detected a chasm between contemporary culture and supposedly contemporary forms of church. This represents substantial overlap with *post-church* groups: one researcher asks if alt.worship is, in part, a therapy group for disillusioned post-evangelicals.

Post-evangelical and post-charismatic elements are significant, but many alt.worship groups have also drawn appreciatively on resources from different traditions: 'Celtic' spirituality (mediated especially through the Iona community); the music of Taizé; the contemplative tradition; creation spirituality; Anglo-Catholicism; and feminist and liberationist hermeneutics. What is striking is the eclecticism of alt.worship, which blends, juxtaposes and remixes ancient forms and contemporary culture. Computer graphics, video loops, photographs, dance, icons, labyrinths, chants and ambient music interweave. Alt.worship is not a return to inherited worship but a creative contextualisation of elements which resist being pigeon-holed or restricted.[138]

But we should not focus only on distinctive components of alt. worship events. The communities that plan and host these embody other challenges to inherited (and some emerging) churches. Many value an understanding of mission that transcends evangelism; an approach to faith that encourages questions, mystery and journeying; an environment where issues of theology, social justice and ethics can be discussed freely and non-judgementally; a non-dogmatic, hospitable and gender-inclusive community; and support for engagement with environmental and global issues. At its best, alt.worship represents a serious attempt to develop a holistic and earthed spirituality.

'*Sanctus 1* is an emerging church based in the city centre of Manchester. We are engaged in a journey of creative exploration into faith, spirituality, worship and community. It is hoped that the Christian community that emerges will challenge both the culture and the church.

'We are an inclusive community and believe that God is not defined by theology. We welcome dialogue between different theological positions but also recognise that dialogue involves listening and real listening involves change.

'We believe that God is already in the world and working in the world. We recognise God's indefinable presence in music, film, arts and other key areas of contemporary culture. We wish to affirm and enjoy the parts of our culture that give a voice to one of the many voices of God and challenge any areas that deafen the call of God and hence constrain human freedom.

'Experience is vital and experience defines us. We aim to provide an environment in which people can experience "the other". In which the vastness of God can be wondered at whilst reflecting on the paradox of the human who was God, Jesus.

> 'We believe in holistic faith. Our worship should reflect and involve this holism and allow freedom to explore new ways in which to wonder at God. We draw from the vast resource of the Christian spiritual journey and are not afraid to look into the past to find a way into the future.'[139]

Can we interpret alt.worship as a post-modern expression of church? Engaging with post-modern culture has been important in its emergence, and some participants are explicit about their missionary encounter with contemporary culture. Their exploratory hermeneutics, participatory ethos, grass-roots orientation, wariness of leadership, non-judgemental inclusivity, playful seriousness, lack of interest in numerical growth[140] and reticence about self-promotion all point towards a post-modern approach to church as well as worship. The sampling and splicing in alt. worship events can be interpreted as a sophisticated engagement of gospel and culture.

But is alt.worship 'church'? We have referred to 'groups' and 'communities' who plan and host worship events, because it is unclear whether they are churches. Some have emerged from inherited churches as 'alternative services' and remain relationally and/or institutionally linked to those churches; others are more independent. But most alt.worship events happen only monthly, although the groups meet more often to plan together and interact informally. For some people, this community is church; for others, it is one expression of church.

Comparing Britain and New Zealand is interesting. In New Zealand alt.worship is mainly Baptist and weekly; in Britain it is mainly Anglican and monthly. With monthly events active participation occurs in the planning rather than in the events themselves; but weekly events involve more spontaneous participation. Groups with a monthly rhythm may struggle to sustain pastoral care and stimulate growth in discipleship; this makes it harder for newcomers to join or know how to become more involved. Groups with a weekly rhythm may function more fully as churches, especially those that integrate creative worship events with other dimensions of community life.

Moot is an emerging church in central London. Its founder was involved in alternative worship groups and some aspects of this church justify placing it in this category. Its style of worship, ethos and interest in the arts are familiar in alt.worship circles.

But *Moot* can also be described as a network church and its mission focus is stronger than many alternative worship groups. It is engaging with pre-churched as well as de-churched and post-churched people. There is also a stronger emphasis on Bible study, albeit with a communal hermeneutic than coheres with alternative worship values.

And what is emerging – and drawing people from the margins – is not just a worship event but a new church.[141]

Some aspects of alt.worship, despite limited interaction with this tradition, are very congenial to Anabaptists (multi-voiced participation, consensual leadership and community herme- neutics), suggesting these developments are significant also for the church's engagement with post-Christendom. But partici- pants and observers also acknowledge various dangers:

- Uncritical adoption of post-modern cultural values that might parallel the uncritical adoption of modernism by many inherited churches.

- Introspection, angst and reactivity in groups formed from those disillusioned by other churches – although this is now less apparent.

- Abuse and manipulation in communities where reluc- tance to grapple with issues of leadership, power and accountability offer limited protection.

- Individualism and self-centredness in multi-directional worship and usually homogenous groups.

- Introversion, given the aversion in some groups to mission and especially to evangelism.

- Exhaustion, given the effort needed to plan and host alt. worship events. The parallel here is with the otherwise very different seeker-oriented church.

- Irresponsible pillaging of the past. 'Post-modern eclecticism comes at a cost. We do a deep disservice to worship and ritual if we dislocate them from their context.'[142]

Culture-specific worship

Alt.worship is not the only expression of emerging church energised by re-imagining worship. Nor does such worship attract a particularly wide range of people, although elements of alt.worship are permeating inherited churches and other emerging churches. Although the age range has broadened since the early years, alt.worship communities comprise mainly white, middle-class, educated Christians. But in a plural culture, no expression of worship will be universally accessible or culturally appropriate.

Mono-ethnic church
By far the largest manifestation of emerging church in Britain (measured by number, size or diversity) comprises a very different membership. These are the burgeoning mono-ethnic churches fast becoming the predominant form of church in many inner-city areas – Nigerian, Ghanaian, Zimbabwean, Congolese, South African, Portuguese, Korean, Chinese, Burmese, Brazilian, Hispanic, Iranian, Punjabi, Tamil and many, many more, alongside longer-established Caribbean churches.

Should these be designated 'emerging church'? Some would demur. The ecclesiology is often traditional and their ethos different from other emerging churches. Indeed, the charismatic fundamentalism, authoritarian leadership and prosperity theology evident in some of these churches are uncongenial to many inherited and emerging churches. A different objection is that including them seems almost condescending; we cannot do justice to their diversity or impact on urban Britain. Numerically, other emerging churches pale into insignificance. Missiologically, these churches are signs of hope in communities where most inherited and emerging churches are struggling to incarnate the gospel.

The inclusion of these churches is an important reminder to inherited churches and other emerging churches that white Christians alone will not effectively incarnate the gospel in multi-ethnic Britain. We must interpret emerging western churches in light of the global church (within which all western churches are now marginal). Including mono-ethnic churches is an invitation to explore partnership, especially in multi-ethnic urban areas that present the greatest mission challenge.

These churches also raise again the thorny issue of homogeneity that has surfaced in earlier chapters. They are sometimes dismissed as homogeneous and thus inauthentic. But most British churches (inherited and emerging) are quite homogeneous; and some churches that began as mono-ethnic are now wonderfully heterogeneous.

An inner-city church in London, less than a decade old but with over 2000 members, from which a dozen further churches have been planted, was started by Ghanaians who continue to lead the church.

It has almost no white members, so some may label it homogeneous; but at the last count there were thirty-four nationalities in the church (twenty-four African and ten Caribbean)!

The church holds services in more than one language and sees it mission as embracing people from all nations in the multi-ethnic community where it is located.[143]

Is 'mono-ethnic church' an appropriate term? Many white churches are equally mono-ethnic! Other terms have been used, none commanding universal assent. Particular churches can be designated Chinese churches, Arabic churches, Nigerian churches or whatever. 'Black church' or 'Black-majority church' sometimes describe churches comprising mainly African or Caribbean members. 'Mono-ethnic church', whatever its limitations, embraces a wider range of churches. It is preferable to 'ethnic minority church', as many are larger than neighbouring congregations and in areas where white people are the ethnic minority. In London today less than fifity per cent of church members are white![144]

If we are to include mono-ethnic churches, why here? The missional dynamic in many of these churches would justify placing them in a mission chapter. Many, though not all, mono-ethnic churches display an evangelistic passion hard to match in inherited or other emerging churches. Some have a more holistic praxis of mission. We could interpret them as further examples of 'incarnating church into different cultures', building communities of faith along relational network lines. We could also place them in the community chapter: providing a place of belonging and cultural identity has been a critical component in their development.

But these churches belong here. A primary factor in their emergence is the desire of participants to worship using their heart language and a style that enables them to encounter God within their own culture. In different churches the language and cultural forms differ and (as cultures are neither hermetically sealed nor static) these evolve through external influences and internal development. But these churches offer their members and others within the same ethnic community spiritually energising and culturally attuned forms of worship.[145]

What are the alternatives to emerging churches with culture-specific worship? We will investigate below attempts to develop multicultural churches or diverse worship within one church. But often the only alternative has been membership of churches unwilling to adapt the worship style of the dominant culture or embrace other spiritual or cultural traditions. This is neither spiritually sustaining nor missionally effective. If we consider culture-specific churches illegitimate, inherited and emerging churches must respond more creatively and radically to the challenges of multi-ethnic post-Christendom.

Two emerging issues for culture-specific churches, however, are their sustainability in subsequent generations and their capacity to recruit from other ethnic groups. It is now evident in some churches that a style of worship (and language) designed by and for those who came to Britain from elsewhere is less attractive to the next generation. Those born in Britain participate more readily in less culture-specific churches. Many are also marrying outside their community. An important development, therefore, are events such as 'Sanctuary in the City', held monthly in central Birmingham and led by Pall Singh of the East+West Trust. These draw on diverse cultural influences and represent a form of alt. worship set in the British Asian context.

Furthermore, many mono-ethnic churches are passionately concerned to evangelise others from different ethnic groups but are aware their services seem uncongenial. Conversations with leaders of African churches reveal a deep sense of responsibility for evangelism in areas where the decline of inherited churches has left them as the primary representatives of Christianity. But there is frustration at the lack of progress: other ethnic groups (especially white people) either resist their evangelistic methods or do not come twice to their services. One African church banned the public use of any language except English in order to be more inclusive, but more radical changes will be needed for multi-ethnic churches to emerge from mono-ethnic churches.

Assessing the advantages and disadvantages of culture-specific worship is a quandary for inherited, emerging and mono-ethnic churches alike, so consultations would be beneficial.[146] The experience of missionaries and mission agencies could also be useful. Questions facing mono-ethnic and other churches in Britain today have parallels with (though also differences from) questions faced by those planting churches in other nations or wrestling with issues of indigenisation and cultural adaptation.

Contextual liturgy

Culture-specific worship is significant not only for mono-ethnic churches but for churches operating within the dominant culture. Urban churches have been alienated by the predilection of song-writers for rural imagery. Working-class churches struggle with the book-based liturgies, wordiness and abstract concepts middle-class churches find congenial. Contextual liturgy earths worship in the thought-forms, language, ethos and rhythms of the local community.

Visiting Australia I discovered the Eurocentricity of inherited liturgy. The 'church year' and associated liturgical resources assume a European calendar. Christmas falls in midwinter and is celebrated with the imagery of candles flickering in the darkness. Easter falls in spring and is celebrated with language of new life and new beginnings. But in Melbourne, Christmas is celebrated with beach parties in midsummer and autumn is approaching at Easter. The 'Australianising' of liturgy associated with the church year means finding appropriate contextual imagery – such as the blaze of judgement associated with Advent. Australians are also producing contextual translations of the Bible.[147]

Contextual liturgy has been important for alt.worship communities, who have adapted inherited resources in light of their local and cultural context, and for culture-specific churches.[148] It is crucial also in indigenous neighbourhood churches, where the development of what Ann Morisy calls 'apt liturgy' enables churches to connect with the spirituality of the wider community.[149] But the challenge of developing contextual liturgy confronts all churches. This does not mean abandoning inherited liturgies that have sustained generations of Christians and, at least symbolically, unite the global church. But it means recognising the influence of Christendom which has exported as normative and transcultural what began as local and contextual forms of worship. And it means finding a balance between the global and the local.

Customised worship

Another approach to issues of worship and culture that affirms diversity but avoids division is the development of customised worship. Some churches recognise the legitimacy of different cultural expressions but resist homogeneous groups and fragmentation. They have encouraged various forms of worship within their existing ecclesial framework. This approach is demanding and normally limited to larger churches.

Multi-congregational church

Many larger churches have expanded through adding further services so more people can use their premises than could otherwise. Adding a second service each Sunday mornings places strain on facilities and requires good time-keeping but enables a growing community to continue growing without huge expenditure on buildings. Although the intention may be to hold duplicate services, so that members can attend either service, this approach opens up new possibilities. Different people may have responsibilities in each service, which may gradually diverge in style or ethos.

Sometimes the intention is to encourage different styles. The earlier service is often more 'traditional' and the latter more 'contemporary', 'relaxed' or 'all-age'. Where this is so, two congregations begin to emerge within one church. How these relate together and continue to be one church varies according to the context. But a single mission statement, joint services, common leadership, shared facilities and finances, cross-congregational home groups, continuing friendships and projects supported by both congregations can help keep the church united.

Some churches have built on the experience of duplicate services and adopt a multi-congregational approach. Since many churches only connect with certain segments of the community, developing new and different congregations might connect with other segments without planting a separate church.

Customised worship takes place in congregations with distinctive cultural styles and practices. Often differences between the two or more congregations are limited, but sometimes more radical differences emerge, as youth congregations or alt.worship communities take shape. Sometimes ethnic congregations also emerge. Within the same ecclesial framework, then, and usually though not always on the same premises, a church operates through several congregations. Each has a distinctive style of worship, mission focus and community expression.[150]

Holding these congregations together more than nominally becomes harder as their number and diversity increase, but this model offers an alternative to the proliferation of culture-specific churches. It also facilitates cross-fertilising and growth in maturity through links with people who are different in age, ethnicity, interests and priorities. An interesting and unexpected result of this multi-congregational approach may be that traditional congregations also flourish.

Two recent conversations with ministers were almost identical. Both had introduced a second Sunday morning service: a traditional service for older members preceded an all-age more contemporary service. This was partly to relieve pressure on the facilities as numbers were growing, partly to reduce tension between members over different styles of worship.

Both ministers were personally committed to the later congregation, expecting this to thrive while the earlier congregation dwindled. Their creative energies were directed towards the later service, though they faithfully maintained the earlier one for those who wanted this.

Both expressed frustration that, despite this, the traditional congregations not only refused to die but were

113

actually growing! Discussing this, it was evident that resolving the 'worship war' through developing two different congregations had encouraged members of the earlier congregation, knowing now what form the service would take, to invite friends. Perhaps, I suggested, both congregations could be growth points for the church, operating through customised worship.

A different (but intriguing) way of sharing resources, but without attempting to be one church, was reported recently:

'Construction has begun in Amsterdam of a multiplex church centre with five worship areas to be used by at least fifteen groups in a suburb that has the country's highest number of immigrant churches. The beginning of building work on 6 July heralded the start of a determined effort to ease the chronic shortage of worship space for Christians belonging to the more than eighty immigrant churches in the Bijlmer suburb of Amsterdam.'[151]

Menu church

Other churches offer customised worship without adopting the multi-congregational approach. Resisting division into linked but increasingly separate congregations, but eager to offer diverse expressions of worship, teaching and community, they provide different forms of church within a single ecclesial framework. Sometimes known as 'menu church' or 'portfolio church'[152], this may involve parallel streams of worship and teaching on the same theme but in different formats. Church members participate in these without losing their identity as members of one community, or choose various activities before a concluding united act of worship.

The Baptist Times reported on 'the church with choice', a community church offering nine 'zones' in its morning service (prayer, teaching, counselling, discussion, praise, quiet, fellowship, children and teenagers). After café-style refreshments, everyone disperses into

the zones, free to move between them until everyone
gathers again for prayer, praise and communion.[153]

Alan Evans of Holme United Reformed Church,
Bradford reports:

'We are aiming to offer people a range of activities,
which will take place in different areas of the building at
the same time. These will include quiet prayer, personal
ministry, drinking coffee, talking or joining the main
church worship. Apart from a central section in which
everyone will be together, they will be able to choose
from a menu of other things.'[154]

As with multi-congregational church, this requires churches
with enough people and resources to sustain a multi-track
approach. It is already familiar within large events, such as
Spring Harvest, which offer a menu of seminars, celebrations,
workshops and other meetings. Experience will show whether
this will prove more effective than multi-congregational church
– or develop inexorably into this.

Multicultural church

Some regard both multi-congregational and menu church as inadequate in light of the fragmented nature of contemporary society,
the demolition of barriers that is a crucial component in the
gospel of reconciliation Christians proclaim, and the eschatological vision of all tribes and people united in worship around God's
throne. For theological and missiological reasons, some argue,
churches in a multi-ethnic society should not endorse or enhance
existing divisions. Homogeneous churches are more comfortable and grow rapidly in the short term, but the gospel requires a
more holistic approach and in the long run such churches may be
unsustainable as well as illegitimate.

This persuasive argument is, however, rarely accompanied by
working models of what it advocates. There are numerous multi-
ethnic churches in Britain – some with multiple ethnic groups
represented, others with two or three main groups – and some
claim to be multicultural; but in most a dominant ethnic group
establishes the cultural norms. Some are working hard to include

members of various ethnic groups in all aspects of church life; some are learning songs in other languages; some are grappling with issues of power and control. I recently encountered a 'simple English' (reduced vocabulary) multi-ethnic church. But, especially in churches with many ethnic groups, the struggle continues: how can they include and value cultures without tokenism or 'melting pot' multiculturalism?

Multiculturalism is a disputed concept in western society. Wale Hudson Roberts, reflecting on the challenge of developing truly multicultural churches, affirms the importance of this but recognises difficulties of definition as well as practice. 'The multicultural church, for all its popularity and ubiquity, however, is still without a coherent definition.'[155] This is a challenge for many emerging churches, not just those working in particular ethnic communities, as homogeneity and culture-specific forms are currently dominant. Postings on emerging church websites indicate some are conscious of this challenge and critical of emerging churches that simply endorse the cultural status quo. They advocate crossing boundaries rather than operating within affinity groups.[156]

Developing multicultural church is an ongoing challenge for inherited churches, too, whatever the commitment in principle to inclusivity and heterogeneity. Inherited churches lack credibility when they criticise homogeneous emerging churches unless they make strenuous efforts to turn theory into practice. Whatever the fine intentions, churches will make little progress until their leadership is multi-ethnic and becomes intentionally multicultural. The changes required to become truly multicultural may mean some church members opting out, feeling they have lost 'their' church.

An Australian church, eager to be truly multicultural rather than dividing into ethnic congregations or expecting its mixed congregation to be assimilated into a uniform and homogenised culture, could afford one staff member. Its creative response was to employ six people for one day a week, each from a different cultural group in the congregation. If we are serious about developing multicultural churches, such radical decisions may be needed!

New monasticism

But re-imagining worship cannot be restricted to what happens when Christians meet together, however creative or customised such gatherings are in emerging churches. Re-imagining worship involves fresh thinking about daily spirituality and rhythms of living. For many in emerging churches, an evangelical 'quiet time' no longer provides the necessary sustenance. There is growing interest in liturgical resources from other traditions, including embracing a rule of life similar to that in monastic communities. As with alt.worship, this does not mean reviving ancient forms of inherited church, but remixing old and new elements. Some discern a new monasticism emerging.

Dispersed church

Some Christians are deeply committed to dispersed church, a community with shared values and a rule of life. Participating regularly – alone or with others – in a daily office that expresses these shared values sustains them and binds them more closely to this community. A well-known example (connected with Building Bridges of Hope) is the Northumbria Community,[157] but there are several others.

'The Quest Community, set up in Glastonbury in 1993, is a wholly dispersed community of Christians from a variety of different denominations who live in their own homes but meet together often for prayer, work and study and to share and offer hospitality and a listening ear.

'At the centre of its life are the daily prayers said at noon in the medieval chapel in Magdalene Street in the heart of a town that has become a mecca for New Age travellers and seekers of every kind.'[158]

Dispersed church usually has a focus, a mother house, a location where members gather periodically, though *I-church* (the Oxford web church) does not. But the rule of life and rhythm of worship build the community. Celtic spirituality has been a fruitful resource for several dispersed churches. In *I-church*, spirituality is nurtured through members making 'a rule of life commitment to prayer, study and action.'[159]

Involvement in dispersed church does not preclude participation in 'gathered' church (indeed, it may stimulate deeper
participation), but for some dispersed church is their primary
community.

Common-purse communities

Another form of new monasticism is the emergence of common-
purse communities, also with rules of life and daily rhythms of
worship, but living together rather than in dispersion and sharing
their possessions and resources. For these Anabaptism, which has
been interpreted as a radical monastic movement,[160] has been an
inspiration or resource:

- A long-established expression is the Society of Brothers
  (Bruderhof) in East Sussex and Kent.[161]

- A different example is the Jesus Fellowship, with common-
  purse community houses in different parts of Britain,
  which (despite notoriety and criticism) reaches people on
  the margins few inherited or emerging churches reach.[162]

- In Australia the Holy Transfiguration Community is a
  remarkable blend of Baptist, Eastern Orthodox and Anabaptist spirituality, with a common-purse and celibate
  community at its heart.

New monastic orders

A third form of new monasticism is the emergence of new
monastic orders, usually with a mission focus. Throughout
European church history monastic mission orders have arisen in
response to contemporary challenges, so it is encouraging some
are responding in this way to the challenge of mission in post-
modernity and post-Christendom.

The *Order of Jacob's Well*, based in Cwmbran, is an ecumenical order drawing on the resources of catholic,
evangelical and charismatic spirituality, primarily
focused on healing and wholeness.

It has a rule of life, aims and vows; it comprises 'along-
siders', candidates, intercessors and licensed ministers.
It has annual conference days and a voluntary prayer
cycle but operates primarily as a dispersed community
with local prayer centres – 'wells'.

Its website insists: 'The Order is not a substitute for, nor does it denigrate the church. Rather, it offers members a "new way of being church".'[163]

The *Order of Mission,* based at St Thomas Crookes, Sheffield, was instituted in 2003 as a global missionary order, a contemporary equivalent of missionary orders.

With a rule of life embracing simplicity, purity and accountability (a revised version of poverty, celibacy and obedience), the Order has a pattern of life with five daily prayer times and an annual conference. Its focus is on missional leadership and church planting.[164]

This Order of Mission is not designed to replace other church commitments but is a conscious attempt to recalibrate church for a new missionary environment.

Boiler Rooms

A final expression of new monasticism is the 24-7 youth prayer movement that began in Chichester in 1999 as a round-the-clock payer meeting and has spread across and beyond Britain. Alongside multiple prayer groups in diverse locations, '24-7 boiler rooms' have emerged in various locations,[165] 'houses of prayer, mission, art and pilgrimage modelled on the ancient Celtic Christian communities and sometimes described as "millennium 3 monasteries".'[166] The Reading boiler room involves over 200 young people, some of whom are still exploring faith. It has several components: continuous prayer, creativity, serving the poor, mission, community, pilgrimage and, since January 2005, a monastic 'rule'.[167]

According to the main website, 'a 24-7 Boiler Room is a simple Christian community that practices a daily rhythm of prayer, study and celebration whilst caring actively for the poor and the lost.

'A 24-7 Boiler Room exists to love God in prayer and to love its neighbours in practice. These purposes are contextualised in community and expressed in a defined location

'At the heart of every Boiler Room is a living community committed to being: 1. Authentic: True to Christ. 2. Relational: Kind to People. 3. Missional: Taking the Gospel to the World.'[168]

Some are convinced a new monasticism is crucial. Andrew Walker writes: 'We will have to return to structures . . . akin to the monastery, the religious community and the sect . . . we will need to create sectarian plausibility structures in order for our story to take hold of our congregations and root them in the gospel.'[169] Tom Sine insists: 'we will need to aggressively work for the re-monking of the church to enable followers of Jesus Christ to intentionally set the focus and rhythm of their lives out of biblical calling instead of cultural coercion.'[170] And Ian Bradley asks: 'Could it be that in the post-modern, pick-and-mix spiritual supermarket we now inhabit, people are actually craving commitment, discipline and obedience?'[171] The increasing popularity of visits to monasteries, pilgrimages and spiritual direction suggest this may be so.[172]

These examples of new monasticism are further instances of emerging churches that transcend our categories of mission, community and worship. They also span the inherited/emerging church divide as new expressions of ancient forms of church. Whether they will thrive and proliferate or be short-lived experiments will be unclear for some time, but they may offer ways of sustaining spirituality, inspiring counter-cultural discipleship and enabling creative mission in contemporary culture.

8

Changing Churches, Changing Mission?

This final chapter will not attempt a definitive critique of emerging church, any more than previous chapters offered comprehensive coverage. It is too soon to assess the significance of specific examples, developing models or the whole emerging church phenomenon. We will identify issues emerging churches may want to consider. But our main focus will be on lessons for the inherited churches to which most Christians still belong.

In an earlier book on emerging churches, Anne Wilkinson-Hayes and I concluded: 'The theological challenges to our ecclesiology represented by the stories we have told are challenges that will face increasing numbers of churches . . . These stories do not provide us with all the answers or even all point us in the same direction, but they may help us recognise some of the important questions.'[173] Emerging churches pose important questions. Scattered across the ecclesial landscape are clues to becoming missional communities in post-Christendom.

Not proven

Scottish law allows 'not proven' as an alternative to guilt or innocence. It recognises situations where inadequate evidence precludes certainty but suspicion remains. As yet emerging churches are 'not proven' missiologically or ecclesiologically. Are they:

- Reinventing the wheel?
- Rearranging the furniture?
- Rejecting the heritage?
- Recycling the disenfranchised?
- Renewing the vision?
- Refocusing the energy?
- Rekindling the imagination?

- Reorienting the community?
- Redirecting the mission?
- Repositioning the church?

Previous chapters indicate issues on which 'not proven' is currently applicable:

- Their capacity to attain dynamic balance between worship, community and mission.
- Their capacity to transform the ethos, not just the shape and style, of churches.
- Their capacity to sustain faith and discipleship beyond one generation and to be reproducible beyond particular examples.
- Their capacity to foster mature communities that can transcend initial homogeneity.
- Their capacity to avoid drifting back into institutional mode and default ecclesial models.
- Their capacity to reach the pre-churched and anti-churched as well as de-churched, semi-churched and post-churched.

Emerging churches *may* be self-indulgent, introverted experiments catering primarily for bored middle-class churchgoers unsatisfied with naïve theology and banal liturgy. Some may be desperate attempts to breathe fresh life into dying models. Others may be angst-ridden communities of like-minded dissidents united by discontent rather by than a transforming vision. Others again may be tentative forays into unfamiliar territory from which pioneers will return licking their wounds.

On the other hand, emerging churches *may* be forerunners of a great movement of missional creativity that will negotiate the transition into post-Christendom. They may herald an ecclesial revolution comparable to the fourth-century Christendom shift. They may kick-start recovery from decades of decline and incarnate the gospel effectively into communities where it is virtually absent. They may catalyse renewal in church and society across western culture.

How do those involved interpret emerging church? Some dismiss inherited churches and regard emerging church as the only hope for future church. Some champion one model and look askance at others. But many are cautious, self-critical and receptive to challenge. Emerging church is exploratory, desperate, self-absorbed, playful, cynical, relaxed, passionate, provisional, hopeful, open, creative, informal and committed – in bewildering combinations. The humble, self-deprecating attitude apparent in many (if not all) emerging churches is refreshing – something many inherited churches might emulate!

Urban Expression is an 'anti-hype' mission agency. Inviting people to commit at least three years (maybe a lifetime) to catalysing indigenous urban churches, we explain 'freedom to fail' is one of our core values. Our 'sales pitch' is that what we are doing is risky, long-term, unglamorous and probably won't work – but if you want to give it a go . . . [174]

This is a refreshing change from the 'this-is-the-answer' advocacy that has plagued churches in recent years. But the seriousness, even desperation, of many Christians in emerging churches, praying and working for ecclesial and missional transformation, should not be underestimated. In passionate discussion, risky initiatives, theological reflection, multi-directional networking and cultural engagement they are pioneering on behalf of inherited churches facing an uncertain future in a changing society.

How might inherited churches respond? Grateful for the risk-taking and courageous pioneering in emerging churches? Suspicious of their iconoclasm and implied/explicit critique of inherited church? Intrigued or offended by their remixing of ancient and post-modern components? Unconvinced they are not parasitic on inherited church? Hoping for the best but fearing the worst?

But 'not proven' is also the current verdict on inherited church! Proven models from past generations are struggling. Emerging and inherited churches are *all* on a journey out of the safe (but confined) harbour of Christendom into the turbulent and uncharted waters of post-Christendom. Bobbing alongside the ecclesial super-tankers are tiny dinghies. They look vulnerable and unimposing but may be more sensitive to the tides and currents; they can certainly change direction faster.

Cross currents

Continuing with nautical imagery, emerging churches are responding to the cultural transitions identified in Chapter 3 – a turbulent environment with many cross currents making navigation difficult. Emerging churches differ as much from each other as from inherited church; some blend ecclesial elements from widely different traditions. This complicates interpretation and assessment.

The significance of emerging church is not numerical. Except for mono-ethnic and cell churches, there are relatively few examples of most emerging models, and most emerging churches are small. This is unsurprising: many began recently; some are small by design; and their proliferation may hardly have begun. Gerard Kelly warns: 'Experimental groups . . . will often lack the resources, profile or success record of the Boomer congregations. By definition, they are new, untried, relatively disorganized and fearful of self-promotion . . . But don't be fooled. Somewhere in the genesis and genius of these groups is hidden the future of Western Christianity. To dismiss them is to throw away the seeds of our survival.'[175]

But we should not *overestimate* the spread or impact of emerging churches. Although these have generated enormous interest, the numbers involved are limited. Stories are circulated and recycled, giving an unwarranted impression of proliferation. Some disappear as quickly as they appear. Some struggle on, making little impact beyond their core group. Some much-lauded models have very limited appeal. Some pioneer radical initiatives before reverting to inherited patterns. Some implode beneath the weight of internal or external expectations.

Nor should we neglect evidence that some inherited churches are thriving. Cathedral congregations across Britain are growing – some adding new congregations to cope with demand. Traditional services in multi-congregational churches are sustaining existing members and attracting others. And some modernist programme-driven churches, which offer pre-packaged theology and unremittingly joyful songs, are flourishing. Charismatic fundamentalism, high-church anonymity and unchanging liturgy still nourish some people in this transitional era. And encouraging signs of life and hope are evident in many ordinary churches throughout the country.

But we should not *underestimate* the significance of emerging churches. These have developed spontaneously and rapidly; although informal story-sharing and networking has prompted further initiatives, there has been little co-ordination or organisation. Emerging church has provocative similarities to previous renewal movements. David Clark notes: 'at the heart of many of the most creative communal changes in Christian history has lain the small group, gathered, inspired and guided by the light and power of the Spirit.'[176] There is biblical and theological justification for watching the margins with care, since God often inhabits unexpected places.

Nor should we place undue confidence in the persistence and apparent health of some inherited churches. Thriving modernist churches may be refuges temporarily holding at bay contemporary cultural challenges. The growth of cathedral congregations may indicate aesthetic rather than spiritual hunger (a legitimate distinction?), yearnings for stability in a changing society or an undemanding option in a post-commitment era.[177] Traditional services may still suit those for whom Christendom persists, but they may not impact post-Christendom.

Trying to negotiate these cross currents, some commentators place greater emphasis on inherited or emerging church. Michael Moynagh, acknowledging the persistence of older models, endorses emerging church as the primary source of hope.[178] Michael Frost and Alan Hirsch agree,[179] and Building Bridges of Hope (Stage B) notes: 'the best efforts of those using traditional patterns of engaging, nurture and enablement seem to be doing little more than slow down the decline.' Bob Jackson recognises the contribution of emerging churches, but he is more sanguine about the potential for inherited church to adopt 'best practice' models and reproduce their impact.[180] This is also the stance underlying Natural Church Development and similar initiatives to help churches maximise their potential. The authors of *Mission-shaped Church* welcomed Archbishop Rowan Williams' encouragement of a 'mixed-economy' approach.[181]

Now and then

As noted previously, no hard-and-fast dividing line separates emerging and inherited church – all churches are both inherited and emerging. Many factors which stimulate fresh expressions of church are equally relevant to inherited churches, challenging them to 'emerge' in various ways. And many resources emerging churches need are found deep within inherited church traditions.

Both inherited and emerging churches need historical perspective and appreciation of resources available from the past. Some emerging churches, conscious they need to be rooted in older and deeper traditions, have drawn freely, if eclectically, on inherited church. Others have not yet discovered this treasure trove. Inherited churches seem historically aware and connected, but many are culpably ignorant of their own history and are stuck in recent traditions that hinder the recovery of radical and life-giving resources.

One predictable reaction to proposals for change in many churches is: 'we've never done it this way before'. Although it is legitimate to acknowledge a church's ongoing story and to question whether a proposal is coherent with that story, this objection often implies an end to discussion. Such a response hinders learning from emerging church.

An alternative strategy is to find within the inherited tradition resources for renewal and transformation. Many denominations and churches have radical roots. Their early years were exciting and experimental, as previous generations grappled with cultural changes, missional challenges and the need for ecclesial flexibility. But more recent traditions are often less helpful. An effective response to the familiar objection is that actually our forebears did something remarkably similar. Inherited church can emerge renewed from its own past.

Introducing the new Salvation Army movement, *ALOVE*, the brochure describes the Army's origins, especially the story of William Booth, and emphasises the continuity between the inheritance of the past and what is emerging. *ALOVE* is described as 'the Salvation Army for a new generation'. Those inclined to object because 'we've never done it this way before' are challenged to re-connect with their own history and deepest instincts.[182]

Emerging churches need not only resources from the past but historical perspective to avoid becoming disoriented, exhausted by innovating or over-burdened by their own significance. They are pioneering in uncharted territory (post-Christendom and post-modernity are genuinely new mission contexts) but are not the first pioneers in church history. But church history can seem overwhelming. Where might emerging – and inherited – churches begin?

- Although post-Christendom is not pre-Christendom, churches in the first three centuries were marginal communities in a plural society, from which we might learn much.

- Negotiating culture shift, we may learn from other generations who responded to such culture shifts (for instance, the Reformation or the Enlightenment).

- Emerging from Christendom, we may learn from marginal groups (including Anabaptists), once dismissed and persecuted, whose perspectives now seem more pertinent than those of their mainstream opponents.

- Investigating our own denomination or congregation may be productive: there are nourishing resources in the history of many churches and movements.

She came to talk about her Christian organisation's recent staff conference. Intruding into the programme, a word she and others suspected was from God urged the leaders of this movement: 'hold on to your heritage but let go of your traditions'. What did this mean? How should they respond? Discussion led them back to their foundations and raison d'être: how had their core purpose and values been stifled or hindered by more recent practices and policies? How could their roots bring renewal?

We may, though, find treasure in unexpected places. Alt. worship groups have been especially astute in finding and adapting resources from diverse traditions. A word of warning, however: sampling from various sources may unwittingly import into emerging churches incongruent values and perspectives. Not all aspects of 'Celtic' Christianity, for instance, are helpful for developing post-Christendom mission strategies, and over-reliance on Celtic liturgical material may hinder development of a robust and integrated spirituality. Similar health warnings can be placed on many traditions, but these are especially necessary when traditions are adopted uncritically.

Here and there

Emerging – and inherited – churches also need a global perspective. Emerging church (as understood in this book) is a western phenomenon, responses to post-Christendom and post-modernity. But:

- The centre of gravity of the world church is now in the southern continents. Even inherited western churches are marginal globally, although theological influence and power structures within most denominations belie this.

- The continuing decline of western churches – even their virtual eradication – may not be a decisive setback to God's global mission. Neither the survival of inherited church nor the success of emerging church is guaranteed; the future of Christianity depends on neither.

- Decline and desperation increase susceptibility to quick fixes. We must resist the temptation to buy ready-made pre-Christendom or Christendom models, however alluring they look and however effectively they are marketed. North American models must be treated very cautiously. We must learn from the world church but contextualise what we find.

- Almost all emerging churches are overwhelmingly white and middle-class. Matthew Glock suggests an alternative title – 'the emerging church in the white, Anglo, post-modern, post-Christian subculture'.[183] Given the inherited church from which these emerged, this is unremarkable. But in the context of multicultural 21st century Britain, failure to transcend this will be problematic.

- A new factor is the arrival of missionaries from other continents, some to work among people from their own nations, others to repay their debt to 'sending nations', which now need this reverse missionary movement.

Dialogue between such missionaries, cross-cultural mission agencies and inherited, emerging and ethnic churches is crucial. We need each other and all the resources of the world church.

Beneath the surface

Surveying emerging churches as we have done risks conveying the impression that any changes are superficial and stylistic. Though this is sometimes the case, emerging church involves more than this. Beneath the surface are sophisticated cultural debate, imaginative missiological engagement and increasing theological reflection.

Despite their diversity, many emerging churches evince shared theological emphases: for instance, creativity rooted in God as creator; community rooted in God as Trinity; and contextualisation rooted in God incarnate in Jesus.[184] Common features include commitment to a Hebraic (rather than Hellenistic) worldview, which means rejecting sacred/secular dualism; preference for mystery and open-endedness over precise and final formulations; and identification with the life of Jesus and his engagement with his context as the model for their own contemporary incarnational ministry.[185]

Inherited churches sometimes raise concerns about heterodox theology in emerging churches, especially those without theologically-trained leaders or accountability to inherited church representatives. Emerging churches, and their advocates, sometimes respond (resisting the temptation to query the orthodoxy of many inherited churches!) by emphasising their theological conservatism. They may be culturally creative, but they do not want to appear theologically innovative.

This response is understandable but unhelpful. There are encouraging exceptions, but many emerging churches are, in fact, disappointingly conservative in theology. Some remarkably innovative churches on the cutting edge of contemporary culture resist extending their creativity to other areas of theology. Theological conservatism may be more dangerous than heterodoxy to the emerging church. Ecclesiological renewal and missiological potency need undergirding with deeper theological reflection to engage effectively with post-modernity and post-Christendom.[186]

Nevertheless, some fresh thinking is apparent. What follows does not characterise all emerging churches, but these elements are discernible in various groups:

- *The locus of divine activity*: recognising God at work in contemporary culture and beyond the church; affirming whole-life Christianity and discovering God in the ordinary as well as the extraordinary; partnerships with people of other faiths or no faith as a context for divine revelation; and less emphasis on church meetings.

- *The meaning of mission*: re-evaluating evangelical models and assumptions; shifting from centripetal to centrifugal or from attractional to incarnational mission; disconnecting faith-sharing from invitations to church; engaging in various political, social justice and ecological initiatives.

- *The interpretation of Scripture*: adopting practices like *lectio divina* and more communal approaches; emphasising mystery, open-endedness and paradox rather than finality and certainty; questioning traditional doctrines of God and the atonement; and considering fresh perspectives on ethical issues.

- *The nature of church*: emphasising 'dispersed church' rather than 'gathered church'; associating church with community or mission as well as worship; interpreting church in more organic or liquid ways; and replacing multiple formal meetings with practising hospitality and sharing lives (and food).

- *The focus of church membership*: advocating 'centred set' community and open edges with 'belonging' before 'believing'; welcoming difference and operating inclusively; preferring less institutional terms than 'membership'; emphasising shared values not creedal assent; and recognising the power of networks.

- *The values of leadership*: abandoning hierarchical and professional models; recognising women in leadership; deconstructing 'worship leaders'; hosting apparently leaderless events; introducing rotating leadership; developing relational accountability; and empowering younger leaders.

- *The scope of participation*: replacing front-led performances with multi-voiced congregations; exploring alternatives to monologue talks; practising communal hermeneutics and group preparation for events; affirming artists and poets, photographers and sculptors; valuing the contributions of those on the margins; and welcoming lament, anger and doubt alongside celebration.

Given the evangelical and charismatic heritage of many participants, emerging church theology, missiology and ecclesiology represent significant shifts of focus, mood and perspective. Evangelical/charismatic convictions persist in some emerging churches (others are 'post-evangelical' and 'post-charismatic'). But alongside these many other ecclesial traditions and theological perspectives are influential. Blending and blurring theological traditions is evident in many emerging churches, as is the sense of journey and openness to fresh discoveries.

A good example of the ethos of emerging churches in relation to their theology and convictions appears on the website of the Belfast-based *Ikon* community.[187] Before identifying their community as iconic, apocalyptic, heretical, emerging and failing, they write:

'Not only is Ikon still "emerging", it is as many different things as there are people who participate in it and influences that penetrate it . . . Indeed, as a movement which is attempting to come to terms with that which cannot be reduced to words, we operate with a liquid system that celebrates ambiguity, openness and change. A system which is as unambiguous as possible about our ambiguity, clear about our lack of clarity and insightful with regards to our blindness.'

Representatives of inherited church traditions may rightly be encouraged that a new generation is drawing on their resources. But they would be wrong to conclude this presages widespread return to their churches. Something new is emerging, which is recombining elements from many times and places. Actually, emerging churches are challenging inherited churches to investigate the resources within their own traditions for their own renewal and contemporary missionary engagement.

Questions for emerging churches

The past four chapters contain various questions about emerging church. Some relate to specific models; many apply to several kinds of emerging church. Some are often discussed in emerging churches; others less so. They are not intended as judgemental or implying an emerging church model is inauthentic. Revisiting the many models we have introduced and surveying the evolving emerging church, what questions should we underline and what further questions might we pose?

- How do churches maintain the creative tension between being 'culturally attuned' and 'counter-cultural'?
- Which aspects of post-modern culture should churches embrace, and which must be challenged?
- Are some emerging churches so besotted with post-modernity they ignore other shaping influences in contemporary culture.
- What emerging churches are incarnating good news among the poor (who are neighbourhood-based and not particularly post-modern)?
- How seriously is the challenge of post-Christendom taken (or understood) within emerging churches?
- Will distaste for inherited models of evangelism discourage all evangelism, or will new – and effective – expressions emerge?
- Are emerging churches developing inter-generational strategies to pass on the faith in a culture where the Christian story and its values are becoming alien?
- Are emerging church models reproducible, and does this matter?
- In a post-commitment culture, are high-commitment church models needed, or low-commitment models?
- What processes are in place to foster accountable friendships and prevent abuse? Old models of control, risk-aversion and stifling institutionalism are rejected, but it is dangerous to ignore authority issues.
- Does emerging church really represent changes of struc-

ture, location, shape or style rather than changes of values or ethos?

- Has the focus on ecclesial renewal hindered deeper reflection on missiology?

- In moving from inherited to emerging church, from congregations to cells, do the gains outweigh the losses?[188]

We cannot pursue most of these questions, but three issues require further comments.

First, on the cultural attunement/counter-cultural spectrum, most emerging churches emphasise cultural attunement. Although this has provoked charges of syncretism and cultural captivity, this is prejudging young initiatives. As cross-cultural missionaries know, challenging cultural norms from outside is unhelpful; cultural attunement preceding counter-cultural witness is good practice. Post-modernity and its many sub-cultures represent a cross-cultural mission frontier requiring similar patience. If we emphasise counter-cultural witness too soon, relationships will not be established and cultural exegesis will be inadequate for counter-cultural witness. However, counter-cultural witness cannot be delayed indefinitely.

Second, despite understandable distaste for the theology and methodology of inherited evangelism, reluctance to embrace authentic evangelism limits the development of emerging churches. Not only will numbers not increase substantially; communities that are not enthusiastic to share their faith with others stagnate. Furthermore, unless they demonstrate an ability to reproduce through recruiting people other than refugees from inherited churches, they will remain parasitical on inherited church and offer little real hope. As the New Churches discovered, once the supply of transferable Christians dries up, the alternatives are evangelism or demise. Evangelical churches, despite the disdain in some emerging churches, continue to restock the ponds which other traditions (liberal, Anglo-Catholic and emerging churches) fish!

Third, core values are crucial. Centred-set communities can afford open edges only if they have strong centres. The hospitality of many emerging churches is liberating, but around what do people ultimately gather? It is refreshing to ask questions without fear of reproach or simplistic answers, but freedom to ask questions does not imply that every answer is legitimate! There *is* a Christian meta-narrative; there *are* core beliefs and values. Conviction and rugged discipleship are needed for survival, let alone effective witness to Jesus Christ, in post-Christendom.

Challenges for inherited churches

Many of these issues are equally relevant to inherited churches in a changing culture. What further challenges (recognising inherited churches are as diverse as emerging churches) arise from earlier chapters?

- Which emerging church models most or least inspire you, and why?
- Can inherited churches move from attractional to incarnational mode, from cultural imposition to indigenisation?
- What networks and sub-cultures in your area are inherited churches not engaging with?
- How homogeneous is your church and how can it pursue the eschatological vision of a multicultural church?
- In a networking culture and post-denominational church, how can ecumenism be embodied?
- Why are people leaving inherited churches, what attracts some to emerging churches, and how can this flow of refugees be stemmed?
- If many emerging churches are ineffective or uninterested in evangelism, how are inherited churches doing?[189]
- Is it impossible for churches to be effective at *both* attracting converts *and* making disciples?
- How can evangelical and charismatic churches nurture divergent as well as convergent thinkers towards mature discipleship?
- How can churches find a balance between deeply-held core convictions and space for open-ended questions, diversity and mystery?
- How can inherited churches become authentic communities where friendships go beyond 'fellowship'?

- What can inherited churches learn from the worldwide recovery of small-scale church?

- Is there too much emphasis in inherited churches on 'doing church' rather than 'being church'?

- What gifts among church members lie dormant in your church?

- How might the arts and contemporary technology be used more effectively, and what are the dangers?

- How might inherited churches 'remix' historic and contemporary resources to create culturally-attuned worship?

- Are emerging churches rightly suspicious of control structures in inherited churches?

- What can we learn from emerging church models of accountability, multiple participation, apprenticeship and leadership?[190]

- How can risk-taking supplant safety-first inherited church culture, and how are pioneers treated?

Underlying these questions and everything we have explored is the question: what is church, and are our inherited categories and definitions too restrictive? But that takes us beyond the scope of this book.

Let's parley!

So where do we go from here? How do we process these questions and challenges?

Those who have seen *Pirates of the Caribbean* will know the purpose of parleying is to avert unnecessary conflict. Inherited and emerging churches need to parley! Some inherited churches may regard emerging churches as pirates, unauthorised privateers ransacking their treasures and waylaying the unwary. Some emerging churches have little time for structures and processes. But what if the pirates are really pioneers and the processes are necessary safeguards?

Multi-directional parleying might mean:

- Conversations between several groups exploring similar models of emerging church.

- Different expressions of emerging church listening to and valuing each other.

- Emerging churches heeding the concerns and questions of inherited churches.

- Inherited churches learning from the experiences and experiments of emerging churches.

- Inherited and emerging churches engaging in dialogue with church planters and cross-cultural missionaries.

- Pioneers and permission-givers recognising each other's legitimacy.

There are dangers with listening processes – endless analysis, distraction from action, domestication and dilution of radical ideas. But the dangers of not listening in a plural culture where no one expression of church can incarnate the gospel effectively are greater. Emerging churches need the accumulated wisdom of inherited churches; inherited churches need the stimulus of emerging churches.

Parleying is emerging. Consultations, reports and books are introducing inherited churches to emerging church models. Some networks connect particular expressions of emerging church. Others foster interaction between diverse models. Websites offer opportunities for story-sharing and debate. Denominational bodies are sponsoring and accompanying emerging churches. Building Bridges of Hope engages inherited and emerging churches in dialogue.

What might result from such parleying?

- Inherited churches adopting or adapting helpful perspectives and practices from emerging churches.

- Emerging churches learning from history and avoiding repeating mistakes.

- Inherited churches recognising and renouncing attitudes and practices that damage their witness and disable their own members.

- Emerging churches rediscovering and releasing the radical potential of familiar church practices.

- Church planters thinking more creatively about the churches they plant.

- Emerging churches thinking more deeply about themselves and their local context.
- Cross-fertilising between different emerging churches for the benefit of each or even producing healthy hybrids.
- Gaps being discovered – communities or sub-cultures neither inherited nor emerging churches are reaching.
- Inherited and emerging churches forging mutually enriching partnerships.
- New churches emerging from, or out of, inherited churches.
- Both being better equipped for the challenges and opportunities of post-Christendom.

Changing mission?

We return finally to the question of mission. What impact will ecclesial reconfiguring have on our participation in God's mission?

- Emerging church could replace inherited church as the primary agent of mission in a changing culture.
- Post-modern churches could become obsolete as post-modernity is succeeded by post-post-modernity.
- Today's emerging churches may be transitional models opening up ecclesial space for another wave of ecclesial initiatives.
- Emerging church could be another fad that fascinates Christians but bemuses or alienates others.
- Inherited churches could be revitalised through the stimulus of emerging churches and recalibrated as missional churches.

What might 'success' mean for the emerging church? Some resist even asking this typically institutional and modernistic question. Some expect that emerging churches will flourish only for a limited period, perhaps as transitional models preparing the ground for further developments. Some recognise that risky initiatives do not always succeed and value the 'freedom to fail'.

Some anticipate that emerging churches will replace inherited churches. Some hope emerging church values will permeate and transform inherited churches. Some want emerging church to be the means by which we regain the respect of the community and engage in sensitive and effective mission. Some regard emerging church as struggling for the survival of Christianity in western culture.

These are different perspectives on emerging church and its mission! Kelly suggests several may be accurate: 'Many of these new expressions are small and faltering, and some will peter out before they have had time to amount to anything. But others will gain strength and grow to become, for thousands, new points of entry into Christian faith and practice. Only time will prove which are, in embryonic form, the mainstream Christian expressions of the twenty-first century.'[191]

But however we understand the mission of emerging churches or God's mission in the world, it would be tragic if emerging church and the interest it generates became an end in itself. Throughout this book we have refocused constantly on missional issues. Building Bridges of Hope investigates the mission impact of churches it accompanies. The Anabaptist tradition also urges this focus. Our context is missional; we dare not settle for non-missional ecclesial renewal.

This does not mean reverting to unreflective activism or abandoning ecclesial renewal for yet another foray into a society that finds many churches as unconvincing as their message. We need a 'decade of experimentation', not another 'decade of evangelism', and we need to document and learn from successes and failures. In post-Christendom the gospel must be incarnated authentically, and this will require diverse expressions of church.

But emerging churches have yet to demonstrate they are as missionally effective as inherited churches (let alone more effective). This may be their potential, but it is too soon to judge. Until then, emerging and inherited churches – preferably together – must face the challenge of mission in a world where we are all on the margins.

And ultimately, as the Anabaptist tradition has insisted for nearly five centuries, our focus is on Jesus rather than the church. Having begun this chapter with a quotation from *Hope from the Margins*, we end with another. 'What way of being church will reveal Jesus to our society? It would be tragic if we only explored new ways of being church and failed to discover new ways of telling and living the story of Jesus.'[192]

Endnotes

[1] See www.urbanexpression.org.uk.

[2] See Stuart Murray: *Post-Christendom: Church and Mission in a Strange New World* (Carlisle: Paternoster, 2004).

[3] I use this word cautiously, aware that some emerging church people dislike it as implying lack of seriousness in what they are doing. I do not intend this implication.

[4] *Mission-shaped Church* (London: Church House Publishing, 2004), 33-34.

[5] Pete Ward, in Graham Cray et al: *The Post-evangelical Debate* (London: Triangle, 1997), 32-33

[6] John Vincent: *Alternative Church* (Belfast: Christian Journals, 1976).

[7] See Jeanne Hinton: *Communities* (Guildford: Eagle, 1993) and David Clark: *The Liberation of the Church* (Birmingham: NACCAN, 1984).

[8] For a personal account, see Io Smith: *An Ebony Cross* (London: Marshall Pickering, 1989).

[9] John 1:46.

[10] Vincent, *Alternative*, 100.

[11] See further www.anabaptistnetwork.com.

[12] See the bibliography.

[13] See further Stuart Murray: *Church Planting: Laying Foundations* (Carlisle: Paternoster, 1998), 87-108.

[14] *Mission-shaped*, 20.

[15] See further George Lings & Stuart Murray: *Church Planting: Past, Present and Future* (Cambridge: Grove, 2003).

[16] The Philippines.

[17] See fn. 3. The previous report was *Breaking New Ground* (London: Church House Publishing, 1994).

[18] Lings & Murray, *Church*, 16-24.

[19] See Simon Barrow's appendix in Jeanne Hinton: *Changing Churches* (London: CTBI, 2002), 137-138.

[20] Robert Warren has commented that 'the genius of the parish system is that it was a brilliant expression of how to be Church in a non-mobile, hierarchical, feudal society': quoted in John Finney: *Emerging Evangelism* (London: Darton, Longman & Todd, 2004), 112.

[21] The 'network church' will be examined in Chapter 5.

[22] See further Nick Spencer: *Parochial Vision* (Carlisle: Paternoster, 2004).

[23] See further Gerard Kelly: *Retrofuture* (Downers Grove: IVP, 1999), which explores five 'posts': postindustrial technology, postliterate communication, post-modern philosophy, postimperial politics and post-Christian spirituality.

[24] Indeed, for many 'emerging' refers primarily to how Christians are engaging with post-modern culture.

[25] Hence the neologism 'glocalisation'. See, for example, Andrew Davey: *Urban Christianity and Global Order* (London: SPCK, 2001), 24-25.

[26] For an Anabaptist perspective, see Alan Kreider: *The Change of Conversion and*

the Origin of Christendom (Harrisburg: Trinity Press, 1999) and Murray, *Post-Chris-tendom*. For another view informed by but more critical of Anabaptist perspectives, see Nigel Wright: *Disavowing Constantine* (Carlisle: Paternoster, 2000).

[27] For a fascinating survey of the rise of new forms of Christendom elsewhere, see Philip Jenkins: *The Next Christendom* (Oxford: Oxford University Press, 2002).

[28] *Mission-shaped*, 11-12, quoting Callum Brown: *The Death of Christian Britain* (London: Routledge, 2001).

[29] This figure excludes deaths and transfers to other churches.

[30] See further Stuart Murray: *Church after Christendom* (Milton Keynes: Paternoster, 2005), 39-66.

[31] Interestingly, many emerging churches do not include 'church' in their names!

[32] See www.emergingchurch.info.

[33] See Robert Warren: *Being Human, Being Church* (London: Marshall Pickering, 1995).

[34] Some within emerging churches question whether 'church' is a helpful term, given its connotations, but no alternative has yet received widespread acceptance.

[35] See the adaptation of Warren's diagramme in Stuart Murray & Anne Wilkinson-Hayes: *Hope from the Margins* (Cambridge: Grove, 2000), 17.

[36] John 3:8.

[37] George Lings: 'What is "emerging church"?' on www.emergingchurch.info.

[38] Michael Moynagh: *emergingchurch.intro* (Oxford: Monarch, 2004).

[39] *Mission-shaped*, 37.

[40] See Appendix for details.

[41] No attempt is made here to define these slippery terms – what they mean in various emerging churches will become apparent.

[42] See Lee Strobel: *Inside the Mind of Unchurched Harry and Mary* (Grand Rapids: Zondervan, 1993) and Bill & Lynne Hybels: *Rediscovering Church* (Grand Rapids: Zondervan, 1997). For a critique, see Gregory Pritchard: *Willow Creek Seeker Services* (Grand Rapids: Baker, 1995) and Kimon Sargeant: *Seeker Churches* (New Jersey: Rutgers University Press, 2000).

[43] Eddie Gibbs: *Church Next* (Leicester: IVP, 2001), 124.

[44] For details of this model in a British context, read Martin Robinson: *A World Apart* (Crowborough: Monarch, 1992), Paul Simmonds: *Reaching the Unchurched* (Nottingham: Grove, 1993) and Mike Hill: *Reaching the Unchurched* (London: Scripture Press, 1994) or see www.willowcreek.org.uk or www.run.org.uk.

[45] *Mission-shaped Church* (69-70) tells the story of *Explore*, a seeker-targeted church plant from Easthampstead Baptist Church, a recent initiative that is showing promising signs.

[46] For further details, see www.purposedriven.com or Rick Warren: *The Purpose-driven Church* (Grand Rapids: Zondervan, 1995). For a British perspective, see David Beer: *Releasing your Church to Grow* (Eastbourne: Kingsway, 2004).

[47] For further details of cell churches in Britain, see www.celluk.co.uk or read Laurence Singlehurst: *Loving the Lost* (Eastbourne: Kingsway, 2001); Phil Potter: *The Challenge of Cell Church* (Oxford: Bible Reading Fellowship, 2001) or Howard Astin: *Body and Cell* (London: Monarch, 2002). See also *Encounters on the Edge* 3 and 20 (Sheffield: Church Army, 1999 & 2003).

[48] See Carl George: *Prepare your Church for the Future* (Chicago: Revell, 1991).

[49] The wise counsel of Cell Church UK, which emphasises values and discourages unrealistic expectations, has been helpful to many.

[50] See further Steven Croft: *Transforming Communities* (London: Darton, Longman & Todd, 2002).

[51] Building Bridges of Hope researchers recognised this as a significant weakness.

[52] See further www.g12harvest.org, *G-12 Harvest Magazine*, Colin Dye: *Hearts on Fire* (London: Dovewell Publications, 2002) and Ken Gott: *Dismiss the Crowds* (Eastbourne: Kingsway, 2001). Churches in London, Liverpool, Sunderland and Dunfermline have pioneered this model in Britain.

[53] An initiative of the Diocese of Oxford, funding and accompanying several emerging church projects: see www.oxford.anglican.org/page/1498/.

[54] For further information, see www.contemplativefire.org.

[55] Ian Bradley: *Colonies of Heaven* (London: Darton, Longman & Todd, 2000), 4ff. Cf. Spencer, *Parochial Vision*, a book-length argument for minsters. Bradley references Celtic models, Spencer Anglo-Saxon models.

[56] An Anglican Church Planting Initiatives newsletter listed several examples, including 'The Path' in Cheltenham, St Thomas Crookes in Sheffield and Fountain of Life in Norfolk. See also the reference to 'major benefices' in Richard Thomas: *Counting People In* (London: SPCK, 2003), 85.

[57] See www.htb.org.uk.

[58] See www.sttoms.net. Cf. Holy Trinity, Brompton's 'pastorates', although these are not necessarily as mission-oriented as clusters. The recent restructuring of the Baptist Union introduced *clustering* as a way several churches might relate together for mission and mutual support. This is a different use of the term, although such clusters could enable smaller churches to co-operate more effectively.

[59] See further Murray, *Church Planting*, 217-230.

[60] For café churches (as distinct from café-style churches), see chapter 5.

[61] Personal correspondence. For further examples of café-style churches, see Graham Horsley: *Planting New Churches* (London: The Methodist Church, 2001), 24-29; *Encounters on the Edge 7* (2000); and www.regenthall.co.uk/cafechurch/.

[62] 'The workplace will be the neighbourhood of the twenty-first century' claims Leonard Sweet in *Quantum Spirituality* (Dayton: Spirit Venture Ministries, 1994), 174.

[63] This was one of the findings of Building Bridges of Hope Stage B. See further Michael Moynagh, *Changing World, Changing Church* (London: Monarch, 2001), 71-75.

[64] *Encounters on the Edge* 24 (2004). See also www.oasisedinburgh.com.

[65] See www.zacsplace.org.

[66] See www.pubchurch.com and www.emergingchurch.info/stories/barnone/index.htm.

[67] For other examples, see www.pubchurch.co.uk, www.b1church.net and www.ikon.org.uk.

[68] See, among others, Manuel Castells: *The Rise of the Network Society* (Oxford: Blackwell, 2000).

[69] For example, *Echo* in Belfast, supported by the City Centre Clergy Fellowship and Belfast Central Mission. See www.godspace.co.uk.

[70] See www.ngm.org.uk. ngm are also involved in *Contagious*, an emerging club-culture and student church in Bristol.

[71] See www.qpcrypt.com.

[72] Peter Neilson: 'Young People and the City: Reflections on Exploring Church for Club Culture' (paper presented at CCOM Annual Commission Meeting: Glasgow, 14-16 September 2001). Cf. Hinton, *Changing*, 69-71.

[73] See www.ravenlive.info.

[74] See www.cafechurch.org. For further examples (both Sydney-based), see www.marshillcafe.com.au and www.cafechurch.org.au.

[75] Michael Frost & Alan Hirsch: *The Shaping of Things to Come* (Peabody: Hendrickson, 2004), 25.

[76] *Mission-shaped*, 50.

[77] See www.emergingchurch.info/stories/redcafe/index.htm.

[78] Frost & Hirsch, *Shaping*, 24.

[79] Hinton, *Changing*, 25-27, 80-88.

[80] Building Bridges of Hope (Stage B) uses 'faith-sharing' similarly to describe 'an intuition that Christian faith . . . may best develop through joint exploration . . . rather than through a one-sided conversation.'

[81] *Encounters on the Edge* 26 (2005).

[82] See www.northumbriacommunity.org/Crossroads/crossroadsurbanspace.htm and *Encounters on the Edge* 25 (2005).

[83] See (the now dated) Patrick Dixon: *CyberChurch* (Eastbourne: Kingsway, 1997).

[84] British examples include: www.webchurch.org (Church of Scotland); www.CofE.org.uk (run by an Anglican vicar in Tyne and Wear); and www.church.co.uk (Oasis Trust). An attempt to create a 'virtual church' on the Ship of Fools website was launched as this book was nearing completion.

[85] See www.i-church.org.

[86] See further www.netchurch.org.uk and http://b1.mychurchwebsite.co.uk/. See also *Encounters on the Edge* 7 and 19 (2000 & 2003) and *Mission-shaped*, 8, 62-64.

[87] See further www.emergingchurch.info/stories/dnanetworks/index.htm.

[88] See, for example, the story, beliefs and values of a church rooted in the London underground music scene: www.gloriousundead.com. For an example in Manchester, see www.aranights.com, a site which contains resources for reflection on the integration of Christian and Goth perspectives.

[89] For further resources on this approach, see articles in *Evangelical Missions Quarterly* 34:3 (October 1998). For similar ideas in relation to Hindu culture, see www.rethinkingforum.com. The Rethinking Forum 'endeavours to promote the birthing of Christ-centred movements within Hindu cultures and communities.'

[90] Moynagh, *Changing*, 110.

[91] For a leading example, offering further insights also into cyber-church, see www.churchnext.net – the website of *Tribal Generation*.

[92] Graham Cray: *Youth Congregations and the Emerging Church* (Cambridge: Grove, 2002), 15. This booklet precludes the need for a longer section on youth churches. For a detailed study of four youth churches and reflection on their missiological significance, see John Hall: 'The Rise of the Youth Congregation and its Missiological Significance' (PhD thesis: University of Birmingham, 2003).

[93] See Gavin Reid: *To Canterbury with Love* (Eastbourne: Kingsway, 2002), 36. For information about *Children Matter*, a network grappling with this challenge, see http://tahilla.typepad.com/children_matter/.

[94] For one model of children's church, see Geoff Pearson & Philip Clark: *Kids*

Endnotes

Klubs (Cambridge: Grove, 2001). See also www.kidschurch.freeuk.com, the website of Kids' Church in Andover.

⁹⁵ Matthew 18:1-4.

⁹⁶ Cf. Kelly, *Retrofuture*, 72-73. This claim reflects a bias in some emerging church circles.

⁹⁷ See www.unoh.org.

⁹⁸ See www.urbanexpression.org.uk.

⁹⁹ See www.emergingchurch.info/reflection/andrewhamilton/arewethereyet. htm.

¹⁰⁰ Peter Brierley (Ed.): *UKCH Religious Trends 5* (London: Christian Research, 2005), 12.3.

¹⁰¹ See www.alphacourse.org.

¹⁰² Peter Brierley: *The Tide is Running Out* (London: Christian Research, 2000), 175.

¹⁰³ *Mission-shaped*, 61. The report (67-69) also notes the emergence of schools-based churches meeting midweek. See further Ann Morisy: *Journeying Out* (London: Morehouse, 2004), 197-199; Mike Booker & Mark Ireland: *Evangelism – which way now?* (London: Church House, 2003), 166-168 and *Encounters on the Edge* 11 (2001).

¹⁰⁴ See further www.ark-t.org.

¹⁰⁵ See www.churchinwales.org.uk/cmm/renewal/ssandygrimwood.html.

¹⁰⁶ Booker & Ireland, *Evangelism*, 104.

¹⁰⁷ See www.shaftesburysociety.org/downloads/CFEReport.pdf pp3-4.

¹⁰⁸ Chris Erskine: *The Concentric Church* (London: The Shaftesbury Society, 2003).

¹⁰⁹ Murray & Wilkinson-Hayes, *Hope*, 8-9. Cf. *Encounters on the Edge* 1 (1999). This initiative has since developed in other ways, but the story of its origins illustrates the point.

¹¹⁰ Murray & Wilkinson-Hayes, *Hope*, 7-8. Cf. Hinton, *Changing*, 25-27, 45-47. For further examples of churches emerging from community projects, see Hinton, *Changing*, 72-79 and *Encounters on the Edge* 2 and 6 (1999 & 2000).

¹¹¹ Hinton, *Changing*, 62-63. See further Kathy Galloway: *Starting where we are* (Glasgow: Wild Goose, 1998).

¹¹² Hinton, *Changing*, 105.

¹¹³ Morisy, *Journeying*, 185.

¹¹⁴ See further Andy Weir: 'The involvement of new forms of church in the regeneration of deprived communities' (MSc thesis: Sheffield Hallam University, 2002). Weir gives further examples and compares evangelical and liberal approaches.

¹¹⁵ Examples are given in *Mission-shaped*, 155 and Moynagh, *Changing*, 114.

¹¹⁶ Matthew 11:19; Luke 7:34.

¹¹⁷ John 2:1-11; 13:1-16; 21:9-14.

¹¹⁸ Cell churches featured in chapter 4. Jeanne Hinton & Peter Price: *Changing Communities* (London: CTBI, 2003) introduce Christian communities, so we need not include these here. For examples of base ecclesial communities, see www.emergingchurch.info/stories/basecommunities/index.htm and www.stmargaret-marys.org.uk/bec1.html. On home churches and more generally on small-scale church, see Robert & Julia Banks: *The Church Comes Home* (Peabody: Hendrickson, 1998) and Wolfgang Simson: *Houses that Change the World* (Carlisle: OM Publishing, 1998).

145

[119] See www.thecrowdedhouse.org/homesweet.htm.

[120] Booker & Ireland, *Evangelism*, 139.

[121] See www.organicchurch.net. See also www.simplechurch.org.uk and www.simplechurch.co.uk.

[122] See Pete Ward: *Liquid Church* (Peabody: Hendricksen, 2002); and www.ncd-international.org.

[123] See, for example, www.emergingchurch.info/stories/annadodridge/index.htm.

[124] Terminology associated with David Tomlinson: *The Post-Evangelical* (London: Triangle, 1995).

[125] See www.holyjoes.com.

[126] See Alan Jamieson: *A Churchless Faith* (London: SPCK, 2002) and *Journeying in Faith* (London: SPCK, 2004).

[127] Jamieson, *Journeying*, 141, 144. EPC stands for evangelical, Pentecostal and charismatic.

[128] See http://www.opensourcetheology.net/node/view/382.

[129] This approach, familiar in emerging church, derives from Anabaptist anthropologist Paul Hiebert. See Paul Hiebert: *Missions and the Renewal of the Church* (Pasadena: Fuller, 1983).

[130] Some participants dislike the term 'alternative worship', but it has become normative.

[131] Several appear in the Appendix. Among many websites, see especially www.alternativeworship.org and www.smallfire.org.

[132] Steve Taylor: 'A New Way of Being Church' (PhD thesis: University of Otago, 2003), 2. His insights inform this section.

[133] See Jonny Baker, in Pete Ward (Ed.): *The Rite Stuff* (Oxford: Bible Reading Fellowship, 2004), 85.

[134] See Richard Hubbard: 'Common Place or Holy Space' *London School of Theology Review* 2004, 6.

[135] Baker, in Ward, *Rite*, 91.

[136] See further www.vaux.net.

[137] Gibbs, *Church*, 143.

[138] See further Robert Webber: *Ancient-Future Faith* (Grand Rapids: Baker, 1999).

[139] From www.sanctus1.co.uk. See also www.emergingchurch.info/stories/sanctus1/index.htm.

[140] Most alt.worship communities are small (to Pete Ward is attributed the comment that in most groups there are more televisions than people!).

[141] See www.klisia.net.

[142] Ward, *Rite*, 12.

[143] See www.ccbc.org.uk.

[144] Brierley, *Tide*, 139.

[145] An important question we cannot explore here is whether styles of worship, theological convictions and ethical commitments in some ethnic churches owe more to the influence of western missionaries in earlier generations than to the host cultures.

[146] Such as a consultation in London in May 2005 involving many African and Caribbean church leaders, co-sponsored by Building Bridges of Hope.

[147] For resources, see www.laughingbird.net. Cf. the New Zealand Anglican prayer book.

146

[148] Cf. the development of 'Womanchurch' with its carefully vetted feminist language.

[149] Morisy, *Journeying*, 156-164.

[150] See, for example, *Encounters on the Edge* 8 (2000).

[151] In Churches Together in England's *Pilgrim Post* September 2005, 8.

[152] Although 'portfolio church' also describes the phenomenon of Christians choosing not to belong to one church but to sample many.

[153] *The Baptist Times*, 27 May, 2004, 2.

[154] Cited in David Hilborn: *Picking up the Pieces* (London: Hodder & Stoughton, 1997), 50.

[155] Wale Hudson Roberts: 'The Multicultural Society, the Multicultural Church' in Michael Eastman & Steve Latham (Eds.): *Urban Church* (London: SPCK, 2004), 70.

[156] See, for example, www.emergingchurch.info/reflection/geoffholsclaw/index.htm.

[157] See www.northumbriacommunity.org.

[158] Bradley, *Colonies*, 53-54.

[159] See www.i-church.org.

[160] Although only the Hutterites practised common-purse community. See Kenneth Davis: *Anabaptism and Asceticism* (Scottdale: Herald Press, 1974).

[161] See www.bruderhof.co.uk.

[162] See www.jesus.org.uk. See further Trevor Saxby: *Pilgrims of a Common Life* (Scottdale: Herald, 1987).

[163] See www.jacobswell.org.uk. The patron of this order is Rowan Williams, who as Archbishop of Wales also instituted the *Order of Living Proof* based in Cardiff (the story of which is referred to in chapter 6).

[164] See www.sttoms.net.

[165] Reading, Staines, Brighton, London – and others are planned.

[166] See www.24-7prayer.com.

[167] See www.curve.org.uk/rbr.

[168] See www.boiler-rooms.com.

[169] Andrew Walker: *Telling the Story* (London: SPCK, 1996), 190.

[170] Cited in Heather Wraight (Ed.): *They call themselves Christians* (London: Christian Research/ LCWE, 1998), 109.

[171] Bradley, *Colonies*, 55.

[172] As did the remarkable television reality series in 2005, 'The Monastery'.

[173] Murray & Wilkinson-Hayes, *Hope*, 18.

[174] See www.urbanexpression.org.uk.

[175] Kelly, *Retrofuture*, 185.

[176] Clark, *Liberation*, 72.

[177] See further Thomas, *Counting*, 98-105.

[178] Moynagh, *emergingchurch*.

[179] Frost & Hirsch, *Shaping*.

[180] Bob Jackson: *Hope for the Church* (London: Church House Publishing, 2002).

[181] *Mission-shaped*, 26

[182] See further www.salvationarmy.org.uk/alove.

[183] See www.emergingchurch.info/reflection/matthewglock/index.htm.

[184] See further *Mission-shaped*, 84-103 (though this is a theological framework developed by the report's authors).

[185] The writings of N.T. Wright have been particularly influential, as indicated

by the 'Future of the People of God' conference in July 2004, which involved inherited and emerging church representatives dialoguing around his writings.

[186] A hopeful sign is the theological conversation hosted by www.open-sourcetheology.net.

[187] See www.ikon.org.uk.

[188] For example: presence/hiddenness, engaged/distinctive; immanence/transcendence, small/large and permanence/transience. See Murray & Wilkinson-Hayes, *Hope*, 19-22.

[189] According to Building Bridges of Hope Stage B, not well: 'faith sharing between Christians and others is rare'!

[190] Building Bridges of Hope Stage B reported on an over-optimistic view of the reality of team leadership and lay participation/initiation.

[191] Kelly, *Retrofuture*, 183.

[192] Murray & Wilkinson-Hayes, *Hope*, 24.

Emerging Church:
A Tentative Classification

MISSION-ORIENTED

Restructuring churches for mission
Seeker-oriented church
Purpose-driven church
Cell church
G12 cell church
Minsters
Clusters
Café-style church

Importing church into new places
Workplace church
Pub church
Club-culture church
Café church
Enterprise church
Cyber-church

Incarnating church into different cultures
Network church
Culture-specific church
Youth church
Young adult church
Children's church
Church for marginalised groups
Indigenous neighbourhood churches

COMMUNITY-ORIENTED

Churches shaped by community engagement
Midweek church

Project church
7-day-a-week church
Post-Alpha church

Churches shaped by community dynamics
Table church
Household church
Base ecclesial communities
Small Christian communities
Organic church
Post-church communities

WORSHIP-ORIENTED

Alternative worship
Culture-specific worship
Mono-ethnic church
Contextual liturgy

Customised worship
Multi-congregational church
Menu church
Multicultural church

New monasticism
Dispersed church
Common-purse communities
New monastic orders
Boiler rooms

Select Bibliography

Church planting

Carey, George (et al): *Planting New Churches* (Guildford: Eagle, 1991).

Ellis, Roger & Roger Mitchell: *Radical Church Planting* (Cambridge: Crossway, 1992).

Horsley, Graham: *Planting New Churches* (London: Methodist Publishing House, 2001).

Lings, George & Stuart Murray: *Church Planting: Past, Present and Future* (Cambridge: Grove, 2003).

Murray, Stuart: *Church Planting: Laying Foundations* (Carlisle: Paternoster, 1998).

Nodding, Peter: *Local Church Planting* (London: Marshall Pickering, 1994).

Robinson, Martin & Stuart Christine: *Planting Tomorrow's Churches Today* (Crowborough: Monarch, 1992).

Shenk, David & Ervin Stutzman: *Creating Communities of the Kingdom* (Scottdale: Herald, 1988).

Wagner, C Peter: *Church Planting for a Greater Harvest* (Ventura: Regal, 1990).

Emerging church

Astin, Howard: *Body and Cell* (Crowborough: Monarch, 1998).

Baker, Jonny & Doug Gay: *Alternative Worship* (London: SPCK, 2003).

Banks, Robert & Julia: *The Church Comes Home* (Peabody: Hendrickson, 1998).

Beckham, Bill: *The Second Reformation* (Houston: Touch Publications, 1993).

Beer, David: *Releasing your Church to Grow* (Eastbourne: Kingsway, 2004).

Cray, Graham: *Youth Congregations and the Emerging Church* (Cambridge: Grove, 2002).

Croft, Steven: *Transforming Communities* (London: Darton, Longman & Todd, 2002).

Frost, Michael & Alan Hirsch: *The Shaping of Things to Come* (Peabody: Hendrickson, 2004).

Gibbs, Eddie: *Church Next* (Leicester: IVP, 2001).

Gibbs, Eddie & Ryan Bolger: *Emerging Churches* (Grand Rapids: Baker, forthcoming).

Hill, Mike: *Reaching the Unchurched* (London: Scripture Press, 1994).

Lings, George: *Encounters on the Edge* (Sheffield: The Sheffield Centre, quarterly).

Moynagh, Michael: *Changing World, Changing Church* (Oxford: Monarch, 2001).

Moynagh, Michael: *Emergingchurch.intro* (Oxford: Monarch, 2004).

Murray, Stuart & Anne Wilkinson-Hayes: *Hope from the Margins* (Cambridge: Grove, 1999).

Murray, Stuart: *Church after Christendom* (Milton Keynes: Paternoster 2005).

Murray, Stuart: *Post-Christendom* (Carlisle: Paternoster, 2004).

Nazir-Ali, Michael: *Shapes of the Church to Come* (Eastbourne: Kingsway, 2001).

Potter, Phil: *The Challenge of Cell Church* (Oxford: Bible Reading Fellowship, 2001).

Riddell, Mike (et al): *The Prodigal Project* (London: SPCK, 2000).

Riddell, Mike: *Threshold of the Future* (London: SPCK, 1998).

Robinson, Martin: *A World Apart* (Crowborough: Monarch, 1992).

Simson, Wolfgang: *Houses that Change the World* (Carlisle: OM Publishing, 1998).

Singlehurst, Laurence: *Loving the Lost* (Eastbourne: Kingsway, 2001).

Ward, Pete: *Liquid Church* (Peabody: Hendricksen, 2002).

Warren, Rick: *The Purpose-driven Church* (Grand Rapids: Zondervan, 1995).

Mission-shaped Church (London: Church House Publishing, 2004).

Other emerging church resources

Theses

John Hall: 'The Rise of the Youth Congregation and its Missiological Significance' (PhD thesis: University of Birmingham, 2003).

Steve Taylor: 'A New Way of Being Church: A case Study Approach to Cityside Baptist Church as Christian Faith "making do" in a Postmodern World' (PhD thesis: University of Otago, 2003).

Andy Weir: 'The involvement of new forms of church in the regeneration of deprived communities' (MSc thesis: Sheffield Hallam University, 2002).

The Sheffield Centre holds other dissertations, as does Cliff College, Calver.

Reports

Less easy to access, but proliferating, are sabbatical and other reports on emerging church. Denominational research departments and libraries of theological colleges are worth consulting. Gill Poole's report for the Church Mission Society contains many stories.

Websites

Many (but by no means all) emerging churches have websites; 'emerging church' typed into an internet search engine produces multiple results. Some websites act as portals into particular emerging church models. Useful examples include:

www.emergingchurch.info
www.alternativeworship.org
www.emergingchurch.org
www.emergent-uk.org
www.celluk.co.uk
www.accn.org.uk
www.encountersontheedge.org.uk
www.run.org.uk
www.urbanexpression.org.uk
www.organicchurch.net
www.newway.org.uk
www.opensourcetheology.net
www.spirited.net.au
www.emergentvillage.com
www.emergingchurchnetwork.com
www.futurechurch.org.nz
www.freshexpressions.org.uk

Networks

Networks are emerging that link similar or diverse emerging churches. Several of the websites relate to these. British examples include:

Anglican Cell Church Network
Anglican Church Planting Initiatives
Cell Church UK
Cutting Edge (Oxford Diocese)
Emergent
Encounters on the Edge (The Sheffield Centre)
New Way of Being Church
Reaching the Unchurched Network
Urban Expression Associates